DON CONROY
ALAN McGUIRE

THE BIG MOVIE QUIZ BOOK

PLUS Amazing Facts and Trivia

MENTOR
BOOKS

Published by Mentor Books 2004

MENTOR BOOKS
43 Furze Road,
Sandyford Industrial Estate,
Dublin 18.
Tel. (+ 353 1) 295 2112/3   Fax. (+ 353 1) 295 2114
email: admin@mentorbooks.ie
www.mentorbooks.ie

ISBN: 1-84210-282-6

A catalogue record for this book is available from the British Library

Research: David Conroy, Don Conroy, Alan McGuire

Edited by Claire Haugh
Design and Layout by Nicola Sedgwick
Cover Design by Anú Design

Printed in Ireland by ColourBooks Ltd.

1 2 3 5 7 9 8 6 4 2

Answers to questions on back cover:
Richard Roundtree, Jane Campion, Stuart Townsend

Contents

To Gaye and to Paula with love

GENERAL
KNOWLEDGE

Take 1

1 What 2003 comedy starred Matt Damon and Greg Kinnear as twin brothers joined at the hip?

2 Which top comic actor starred in *The Man Who Sued God* (2001)?

3 Complete the title of this 2003 Jim Carrey movie: _____ *Almighty.*

4 Name the 2003 movie that portrayed the true story of climbers Joe Simpson and Simon Yates and their harrowing experience climbing the west face of Siula Grande in the Peruvian Andes.

5 Who played the artist Johannes Vermeer in *Girl With a Pearl Earring (2004)*?

6 What actor received the title Mr Universe in 1967?

7 What was the longest sword fight in screen history?

8 Who said 'Take your stinking paws off me, you damn dirty ape'.

9 Who played the cynical newspaper man in *Ace in the Hole* (1951)?

10 Who played John Steed in *The Avengers* (1998)?

11 Name the 2003 romantic comedy in which the British Prime Minister (played by Hugh Grant) falls in love with his tea lady.

12 Who played the two male leads in *Elf* (2003)?

13 Name the 2003 movie where a mother and daughter wake up in each other's body.

14 Name the 2003 movie about a dog from outer space.

15 Which actor/singer won a 1988 Grammy Award for a rap song 'Parents just don't understand'?

The first cinema was called Cinematographe Lumière and was in Paris in the Grand Café. It opened on 28 December 1895.

Answers

1 *Stuck On You*

2 Billy Connolly

3 *Bruce Almighty*

4 *Touching the Void*

5 Colin Firth

6 Arnold Schwarzenegger. He won the title five times!

7 Between Errol Flynn and Basil Rathbone in *The Adventures of Robin Hood* (1938)

8 Charlton Heston in *Planet of the Apes* (1968)

9 Kirk Douglas

10 Ralph Fiennes

11 *Love Actually*

12 Will Ferrell and James Caan

13 *Freaky Friday*

14 *Good Boy!*

15 Will Smith

'There were three things that my brother Chico was always on:
a phone, a horse, or a broad.'
– *Groucho Marx*

Take 2

1   Former married couple Angelina Jolie and Johnny Lee Miller starred alongside each other in what 1995 cyber tale?

2   *Happy Gilmore* (1996), starring Adam Sandler, portrayed him conquering which sport?

3   Who directed *In & Out* (1997), starring Kevin Kline, John Cusack and Matt Dillon?

4   *The Jewel of the Nile* (1985) was the sequel to which 1984 film?

5   Who played the real-life serial killer Carl Panzram in *Killer: A Journal of Murder* (1995)?

6   Who played the prison warden in *The Last Castle* (2001), starring Robert Redford as the court-martialled three-star general?

7   Sydney Pollack directed Harrison Ford and Kristen Scott Thomas in this 1999 romantic drama involving a plane crash. Name it.

8   Name the 1996 action thriller about a kidnapping, starring Mel Gibson, Renée Russo and Gary Sinise.

9   Woody Harrelson and Juliette Lewis played serial killer lovers glamourised by the media in what 1994 Oliver Stone film?

10 Released in 1986, what was Peter Cushing's final movie?

11 Name the two male leads in Franklin F. Schaffner's prison epic *Papillon* (1973).

12 Who directed the western *The Quick and the Dead* (1995), starring Sharon Stone, Gene Hackman, Russell Crowe and Leonardo DiCaprio?

13 Who directed John Lithgow in *Raising Cain* (1992)?

14 What does Bill Pullman go in search of in Wes Craven's horror flick *The Serpent and the Rainbow* (1987)?

15 In what 1985 film did Michael J. Fox play a werewolf?

'It's a shame to take this country away from the rattlesnakes.'
– *D.W. Griffith (on Hollywood)*

Answers

1   *Hackers*

2   Golf

3   Frank Oz, best known for voicing Yoda and several *Muppet* characters

4   *Romancing the Stone*. Both films starred Michael Douglas, Kathleen Turner and Danny De Vito

5   James Woods. Carl Panzram had the dubious honour of being recognised as America's first serial killer, killing twenty-one people before imprisonment

6   James (Tony Soprano) Gandolfini

7   *Random Hearts*

8   *Ransom*, directed by Ron Howard

9   *Natural Born Killers*, from a story by Quentin Tarantino

10 *Biggles*

11 Steve McQueen and Dustin Hoffman

12 Sam Raimi

13 Brian De Palma

14 Zombie Powder, on behalf of a pharmaceutical company

15 *Teen Wolf*

'All I got from 25 years in Hollywood is three lousy ex-husbands.'
– Ava Gardner

Take 3

1. Name the pair of Oscar winners in *As Good As It Gets* (1997).

2. Jean-Claude Van Damme was in *AWOL* (1990). What does AWOL mean?

3. John Goodman starred in *The Babe* (1992). What sport was Babe Ruth famous for?

4. Chris Rock, Chris Elliot and Phil Hartman starred in what 1993 satirical comedy on both gangster rap and the culture that engendered it?

5. *DOA* (1988) starred Dennis Quaid and Meg Ryan. What does DOA mean?

6. In the 20th anniversary edition of *ET the Extra Terrestrial* (2002) Steven Spielberg digitally replaced the guns being carried by the government officials with what?

7. *54* (1998) starred Ryan Phillipe, Mike Myers, Salma Hayek and Neve Campell. What was the Studio 54 featured in the film?

8. In *GI Jane* (1997) Demi Moore's character became the first woman to do what?

9. Curtis Hanson directed Rebecca DeMornay and Annabella Sciorra in what 1992 'nanny from hell' film?

10. Gregory Peck starred in what Hitchcock movie from 1945?

11. Liam Neeson's first starring role was as a bare-fisted fighter in what 1990 movie?

12. What animal did James Belushi team up with in *K-9* (1989)?

13. Who played the misguided scientist in *The Lawnmower Man* (1992)?

14. Under what title was *Mad Max 2 (1982)* released in cinemas across America?

15. *The Naked Gun* (1988) was a film based on what cult TV series that starred Leslie Nielsen as the wonderfully deadpan cop?

Answers

1 Jack Nicholson and Helen Hunt

2 Absent Without Leave

3 Baseball

4 *CB4 (Cell Block 4)*

5 Dead On Arrival

6 Walkie Talkies. Spielberg did this because of political unrest at the time

7 It was a notorious nightclub in the 1970s

8 She was the first woman to train with the Navy SEALS. The movie was directed by Ridley Scott and starred Viggo Mortensen

9 *The Hand that Rocks the Cradle*

10 *Spellbound*

11 *The Big Man*

12 A dog. The film was made the same year as the Tom Hanks comedy *Turner and Hooch*

13 Pierce Brosnan. The movie also starred Jeff Fahey as Jobe

14 It was released as *The Road Warrior*, starred Mel Gibson and was directed by George Miller

15 *Police Squad!*

At a cinema in Cleveland 150 patrons parked their cars in a 2-hour zone while going to see *Gandhi* (1982), not realising that the movie was 3 hours and 8 minutes long. When they returned all the patrons had parking tickets on their cars. The mayor heard about the incident and voided the parking fines.

Take 4

1   Who played Freddy Kreuger in *Nightmare on Elm Street* (1984)

2   Name Gene Hackman's character in the 1971 movie *The French Connection.*

3   Eddie Murphy played an estate agent in what 2003 horror-comedy?

4   What 2003 movie is a biopic about the comic book writer Harvey Pekar?

5   Who played the female lead in *The House of Mirth* (2000), based on Edith Wharton's novel?

6   Who played bandit Cobra Verde, a slave trader, in the movie *Cobra Verde* (1988)?

7   What 1987 courtroom drama was about a deaf-mute Vietnam veteran, starring Cher, Dennis Quaid and Liam Neeson?

8   Harvey Keitel, Sylvester Stallone and Robert De Niro starred in what 1997 thriller?

9   Who played the lead role as an SAS officer in *Who Dares Wins* (1982)?

10   Who directed the 1969 musical *Hello Dolly*?

11   Name director John Woo's 2001 World War II movie, starring Nicolas Cage and Christian Slater?

12   Which actor played James Bond in *The Living Daylights* (1987)?

13   What 1993 thriller starred Madonna and Willem Dafoe?

14   Complete the title of this 1986 Whoopi Goldberg comedy: *Jumpin'*
_____ _____.

15   Name the third movie (1988) from The Next Generation Star Trek crew.

'My daughter's got a voice like chalk on a blackboard.'
– Judy Garland (on Liza Minnelli)

Answers

1   Robert Englund

2   Jimmy 'Popeye' Doyle

3   *The Haunted Mansion*

4   *American Splendor*, starring Paul Giamatti

5   Gillian Anderson, Eric Stoltz and Dan Akroyd

6   Klaus Kinski

7   *Suspect*, directed by Peter Yates

8   *Cop Land*, directed by James Mangold

9   Lewis Collins. The movie also starred Richard Widmark and was directed by Ian Sharp

10   Gene Kelly. The movie starred Barbra Streisand, Walter Matthau and Michael Douglas

11   *Windtalkers*

12   Timothy Dalton

13   *Body of Evidence*

14   *Jumpin' Jack Flash*

15   *Star Trek: Insurrection,* starring Patrick Stewart

'I am known in parts of the world by people who have never heard of Jesus Christ.'
– *Charlie Chaplin*

Take 5

1   What 1971 Peter Bogdanovich movie was about a small town in Texas and a loss of innocence among its teenagers?

2   Name the 1997 movie, starring Harrison Ford and Gary Oldman, in which the US President's plane is hijacked by communist extremists.

3   Who played the male lead in *The Mackintosh Man* (1973)?

4   Who starred as the would-be nun in *Sister Act* (1992)?

5   Name the 1962 Norman Wisdom comedy in which he plays the dual role of a foreign criminal and a would-be policeman.

6   Complete the title of this comedy from 1961 with Charlie Drake and Cecil Parker: _____ *Pirates*.

7   Lawrence Fishburne, Tim Roth and Andy Garcia starred in what 1997 fact-based film set in 1930s Harlem?

8   A river rescue cop, played by Bruce Willis, hunts down his father's killer in what 1993 movie?

9   Who played the lead in *Rob Roy* (1995)?

10   What 1996 medical thriller starred Hugh Grant and Gene Hackman?

11   Jack Nicholson played an errant classical pianist and son of a wealthy patriach in what 1970 movie?

12   Who directed *Easy Rider* (1969)?

13   Who played an Arab leader at war with the Nazis in *The Wind and the Lion* (1975)?

14   Ewan McGregor, Nick Nolte and Patricia Arquette starred in which 1998 movie set mainly in a morgue?

15   Wife swapping turned into a murder scenario in what 1992 film starring Kevin Kline and Mary Elizabeth Mastrantonio?

'When Ginger Rogers danced with Fred Astaire, it was the only time in the movies when you looked at the man, not the woman.'
– Gene Kelly

Answers

1   *The Last Picture Show,* starring Timothy Bottoms, Jeff Bridges, Cybil Shepherd and Ben Johnson

2   *Air Force One*

3   Paul Newman

4   Whoopi Goldberg

5   *On the Beat*

6   *Petticoat Pirates*

7   *Hoodlum*

8   *Striking Distance*

9   Liam Neeson. The movie also starred Jessica Lange and Tim Roth

10   *Extreme Measures*

11   *Five Easy Pieces*. The movie also starred Melvyn Douglas and was directed by Bob Rafelson

12   Dennis Hopper, who starred alongside Peter Fonda and Jack Nicholson

13   Sean Connery

14   *Night Watch*

15   *Consenting Adults*, directed by Alan K. Pakula

The largest cinema ever, called the Roxy, was built in New York in 1927. It had an original seating capacity of 6,214. Sadly, it closed on 29 March 1960.

The world's largest cinema, the Fox Theater in Detroit, seats 5,041 people. Built in 1928, its restoration began in 1984.

Take 6

1   Who starred in *Mr Saturday Night* (1992)?

2   Who played Lenny Bruce in the movie *Lenny* (1970)?

3   In what 1983 movie did Robert De Niro kidnap a TV host to get his own show?

4   Who was the 'bad lieutenant' in the 1992 movie of the same name?

5   Richard Gere played a lead role in *The Jackal* (1997). Who played the Jackal?

6   A would-be golfer sought guidance from a mysterious person who then became his caddy for a golf marathon. Directed by Robert Redford, what was the 2000 movie?

7   What 1999 movie directed by Woody Allen is the story of a jazz guitarist trying to eke out a living in 1930s New York?

8   Jerry Lewis starred in a 1972 comedy in which he played a comic German. Name the movie.

9   Alec Guinness starred with Gina Lollobrigida in what comedy from 1966?

10 Who played the CIA agent in *Conspiracy Theory* (1997), starring Mel Gibson and Julia Roberts?

11 David Carradine, Simone Griffith and Sylvester Stallone starred in what ultra-violent film from 1975?

12 Who made his directorial debut with *Diner* (1982), starring Steve Guttenberg, Kevin Bacon and Mickey Rourke?

13 Heather Locklear and Stephen Rea starred in what action crime thriller from 1997?

14 In the 1997 movie *A Life Less Ordinary*, Ewan McGregor's character kidnapped his former boss's daughter. Who played the daughter?

15 Who played the womanising local physician in *Eve's Bayou* (1997)?

Answers

1   Billy Crystal

2   Dustin Hoffman

3   *The King of Comedy*, also starring Jerry Lewis

4   Harvey Keitel

5   Bruce Willis

6   *The Legend of Baggar Vance*, starring Matt Damon and Will Smith

7   *Sweet and Lowdown,* starring Sean Penn and Samantha Morton

8   *Ja, Ja Mein General.* Jerry Lewis also directed this movie

9   *Hotel Paradiso*

10   Patrick Stewart. The movie was directed by Richard Donner

11   *Death Race 2000*

12   Barry Levinson. Ellen Barkin made her screen debut in this movie

13   *Double Tap*

14   Cameron Diaz

15   Samuel L. Jackson

'The only good thing about acting in movies is that there's no heavy lifting.'
– Cary Grant

Take 7

1 Who played Tom Hagen in Francis Ford Coppola's *The Godfather* (1972)?

2 Jeff Daniels, Robert Duvall and Mira Sorvino starred in what 2002 historical war drama?

3 Who played 'the hot chick' in the 2002 movie of the same title?

4 Winona Ryder and Ellen Burstyn starred in what moving 1995 drama?

5 Who was the star of the film *Hudson Hawk* (1991)?

6 First-time director Justin Kerrigan directed what 1999 drug and drink-fuelled film, set in Cardiff?

7 Who played LT Bonham in *The Hunted* (2002), co-starring Benico Del Toro and directed by William Friedkin?

8 Who played the killer in the film *In the Line of Fire* (1993), starring Clint Eastwood and directed by Wolfgang Petersen?

9 Who played Nicolas Cage's nagging wife in *It Could Happen To You* (1994)?

10 Who starred in Terry Gilliam's fantasy comedy *Jabberwocky* (1997)?

11 Who played Jack Frost in the 1998 movie of the same title?

12 Which director walked away from directing the film *Joan of Arc* (1999) because she refused to cast Milla Jovovich as Joan?

13 Jet Li and Bridget Fonda starred in what 2001 martial arts thriller?

14 Who played the truth-telling lawyer in the comedy *Liar, Liar* (1997)?

15 Wesley Snipes starred in what 2002 political thriller based on a single mobile phone call?

'The only difference between me and other actors is I've spent more time in jail.'
– Robert Mitchum

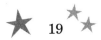

Answers

1 Robert Duvall

2 *Gods and Generals*

3 Rob Schneider, who played cameo roles in many Adam Sandler films

4 *How to Make an American Quilt*

5 Bruce Willis

6 *Human Traffic*

7 Tommy Lee Jones. The movie also starred Connie Nielson

8 John Malkovich

9 Rosie Perez. The movie also starred Bridget Fonda

10 Michael Palin

11 Michael Keaton

12 Kathryn Bigelow. Luc Besson took over the directing and cast his then wife Milla Jovovich anyway

13 *Kiss of the Dragon*. The movie was was scripted by Luc Besson

14 Jim Carrey

15 *Liberty Stands Still*

'I love Los Angeles, I love Hollywood, They're beautiful. Everybody's plastic.
I want to be plastic.'
– *Andy Warhol*

Take 8

1   Finish the title of the Wes Craven horror *The People* _____ _____ _____. (1991)

2   Who wrote the screenplay for *Alien* (1979)?

3   Who starred in the crime thriller *A Rage in Harlem* (1991)?

4   Where do all dogs go according to the 1989 animated film by Don Bluth?

5   Al Pacino and Donald Sutherland starred in what historical war drama from 1985 about the American War of Independence?

6   John Landis directed *An American Werewolf in London* (1981), but what film did he direct in 1980 to both critical and commercial acclaim?

7   Kirk Douglas and Farrah Fawcett starred in what sci-fi adventure flick from 1980?

8   Who played the deceased couple in Tim Burton's horror comedy *Beetlejuice* (1988)?

9   Who played a real-life vampire hired to act in the movie *Nosferatu* in the film *Shadow of the Vampire* (2000)?

10 In *Birdy*, co-starring Nicolas Cage and directed by Alan Parker, what actor played the ex-Vietnam soldier who believed he was a bird?

11 Name the 1994 movie, directed by Jan De Bont, starring Keanu Reeves, Sandra Bullock and Dennis Hopper.

12 Who played bad guy Deacon Frost in *Blade* (1998)?

13 A Prince of Africa became a Prince of Darkness in what 1972 movie, which borrowed the theme from Bram Stoker's *Dracula*?

14 Which Oscar-winning actress starred in the supernatural thriller *Bless The Child* (2000)?

15 Who played Dirk Diggler in *Boogie Nights* (1997), directed by P.T. Anderson?

Answers

1   *The People Under the Stairs*

2   Dan O'Bannon

3   Forest Whitaker

4   *All Dogs Go To Heaven*. The movie was made in Ireland

5   *Revolution*

6   *The Blues Brothers*

7   *Saturn 3*

8   Geena Davis and Alec Baldwin. The movie also starred Michael Keaton, Catherine O'Hara and Winona Ryder

9   Willem Dafoe. The movie also starred John Malkovich

10   Matthew Modine

11   *Speed*

12   Stephen Dorff. The movie also starred Wesley Snipes as Blade and Kris Kristofferson as his sidekick

13   *Blacula*, starring Shakespearean actor William Marshall

14   Kim Basinger. The movie was directed by Chuck Russell

15   Mark Whalberg. The movie also starred Heather Graham, John C. Reilly, Burt Reynolds, Julianne Moore

'It's not funny, what I am is brave.'
– Lucille Ball

Take 9

1   In what 1987 Steven Spielberg film did Christian Bale star?

2   Neve Campbell starred in what (1996, 1997, 1999) horror trilogy?

3   George Clooney and Mark Whalberg starred in what 2000 Wolfgang Petersen film?

4   Stephen Frears directed John Cusack and Jack Black in what 2001 comedy?

5   Name the female lead in *Captain Correlli's Mandolin* (2001).

6   Will Smith starred in Michael Mann's 2001 biopic about the greatest boxer of all time. Name the movie.

7   What silver-haired comic starred alongside Helena Bonham Carter in the black comedy *Novocaine* (2001)?

8   Which *Friends* star appeared alongside Bruce Willis in *The Whole Nine Yards* (2000)?

9   Who starred with Anthony Hopkins in *Instinct* (1990)?

10   Who played the leading role in David Keopp's *Stir of Echoes* (1999)?

11   Haley Joel Osment received a Best Supporting Oscar Nomination for his role in what 1999 film?

12   Jamie Lee Curtis and Donald Sutherland starred in what 1999 sci-fi drama?

13   Who played Willie Beaman in Oliver Stone's *Any Given Sunday* (1999)?

14   Richard Gere and Julia Roberts starred in what 1999 comedy from the director of *Pretty Woman* (1990)?

15   Directors Daniel Myrick and Eduardo Sanchez made a low-budget horror movie in 1999, which became a box office smash. Name it.

When the studio bosses wanted to cut the first *Godfather* movie because they thought it was too long, Robert Evans, the then-producer threatened to walk out. Eventually Paramount agreed not to touch the three-hour saga.

Answers

1. *Empire of the Sun*
2. *Scream 1, 2, and 3*, directed Wes Craven
3. *The Perfect Storm*
4. *High Fidelity*
5. Penelope Cruz. The movie also starred Nicolas Cage and John Hurt
6. *Ali*
7. Steve Martin
8. Matthew Perry
9. Cuba Gooding Jr
10. Kevin Bacon
11. *The Sixth Sense*. The movie also starred Bruce Willis
12. *Virus*. The movie also starred William Baldwin
13. Jamie Foxx. The movie also starred Al Pacino, James Woods, L.L. Cool J, Dennis Quaid and Cameron Diaz
14. *Runaway Bride*
15. *Blair Witch Project*

'There's no formula for success. But there is a formula for failure
and that is trying to please everybody.'
– *Nicholas Ray*

Take 10

1. Matthew McConaughey and Woody Harrelson starred in what 1999 movie about a reality TV show?

2. *The Siege* (1998), a New York political thriller, starred which two actors?

3. Rob Cohen directed *Dragon: The Bruce Lee Story* (1993). Who played Bruce Lee?

4. Who played the female lead in *I:Spy* (2000), starring Eddie Murphy and Owen Wilson?

5. Which *Lord of the Rings* actor co-starred with Heath Ledger in *Ned Kelly* (2003)?

6. George Clooney teamed up again with what film-making duo for *Intolerable Cruelty* (2003)?

7. Before the *Lord of the Rings* triology, Sean Astin and Viggo Mortensen appeared together in what 1985 film?

8. Tommy Lee Jones and Cate Blanchett starred in what 2004 film, produced by Brian Grazer and directed by Ron Howard?

9. Finish the title of this Ben Stiller and Jennifer Aniston comedy film: *Along Came* _____(2004).

10. Tarsem Singh directed Jennifer Lopez, Vince Vaughn and Vincent D'Onofrio in what 2000 sci-fi chiller?

11. Who directed *Pitch Black* (2000) starring Vin Diesel?

12. Name the popular black star of the sci-fi thriller *I, Robot* (2004)?

13. Who played James Joyce in the film *Nora* (1999)?

14. Complete the title of the comedy starring Josh Hartnett: _____ *Days and* _____ _____(2002).

15. Who starred in the 2002 remake of *Rollerball?*

Answers

1   *EDtv*, directed by Ron Howard

2   Bruce Willis and Denzel Washington

3   Jason Scott Lee (no relation to Bruce)

4   Famke Jannsen

5   Orlando Bloom

6   Joel and Ethan Coen. They also directed George in *O Brother Where Art Thou?* (2000)

7   *The Goonies*

8   *The Missing*

9   *Along Came Polly*

10   *The Cell*

11   David Twohy

12   Will Smith

13   Ewan McGregor

14   *40 Days and 40 Nights*

15   Chris Klein, Jean Reno and L.L. Cool J

'Film business? I enjoy the film but the business – that's shit.'
– Oliver Stone

Take 11

1   *Minority Report* (2002), *Total Recall* (1990) and *Blade Runner* (1982) were based on whose novels?

2   Who starred as Bill in *Kill Bill* (2003)?

3   Name the two male leads in *The Fast and the Furious* (2001).

4   Who starred in *School of Rock* (2003)?

5   Who directed *Carrie* (1976)?

6   Who was the lead in *Ferris Bueller's Day Off* (1986)?

7   Who starred as the female lead in Lars Von Trier's *Dogville* (2003)?

8   Can you name the 2003 film in which high school buddies Gene Hackman and Dustin Hoffman appear together?

9   Larry Fessenden starred, directed and wrote the script for what cult vampire movie from 1995?

10 Who played Pindead in Clive Barker's *Hellraiser* (1987)?

11 Who directed *M*A*S*H** (1970)?

12 Name the two male stars in *Carnal Knowledge* (1975).

13 Who directed *All the President's Men* (1976)?

14 *Apocalypse Now* (1979) was a loose adaptation of what Joseph Conrad story?

15 Who was the knight who played chess with death in Bergman's *The Seventh Seal* (1957)?

'Making ET was torture, torture. My pubic hair turned grey.'
– *Steven Spielberg*

Answers

1. Philip K. Dick
2. David Carradine
3. Paul Walker and Vin Diesel
4. Jack Black
5. Brian De Palma
6. Matthew Broderick
7. Nicole Kidman
8. *Runaway Jury*
9. *Habit*
10. Doug Bradley
11. Robert Altman
12. Jack Nicholson and Art Garfunkel
13. Alan J. Pakula
14. *Heart of Darkness*
15. Max Von Sydow

'I believe in censorship – after all, I've made a fortune out of it.'
– Mae West

Take 12

1 What was the Pink Panther in the movie *The Pink Panther* (1963)?

2 Who wrote the theme music for *The Pink Panther*?

3 Name the 1958 movie in which George Nader starred as a Canadian burglar in England. The movie also starred Maggie Smith

4 Name the 1990 movie about the final bombing raid over Germany in World War II, starring Matthew Modine and Billy Zane.

5 Name the two leads in *Men in Black* (1997).

6 Name the 1965 movie in which Charlton Heston, playing a feudal knight, starred alongside Richard Boone.

7 Who played Oscar Wilde in *The Trials of Oscar Wilde* (1960)?

8 Who starred in *A Tribute to a Bad Man* (1956)?

9 Name the 2000 movie starring Rutger Hauer, Ian Holm, Stuart Townsend and Noah Taylor, about a man who claimed to be able to curse crops and speak with the devil.

10 What was the 1976 comedy starring Gene Wilder, Richard Pryor, Jill Clayburgh and Patrick McGoohan?

11 Name the 1985 western starring Kevin Kline, Scott Glenn, Kevin Costner, Danny Glover and John Cleese.

12 What animal was featured in *Ring of Bright Water* (1969), starring Bill Travers and Virginia McKenna?

13 Name the 1959 World War II action movie starring Frank Sinatra, Gina Lollobrigida, Peter Lawford, Steve McQueen and Richard Johnson.

14 Name the 2000 comedy vampire movie starring Jonathon Lipnicki and Richard E. Grant.

15 Peter Brook directed the 1979 movie about the memoirs of C.J. Gurdjieff. What was its title?

Answers

1   A precious jewel

2   Henry Mancini

3   *Nowhere To Go*

4   *Memphis Belle*

5   Tommy Lee Jones and Will Smith

6   *The Warlord*. The movie also starred Rosemary Forsyth

7   Peter Finch. It also starred Yvonne Mitchel, John Fraser, Lionel Jefferies and James Mason

8   James Cagney with Stephen McNally

9   *Simon Magus*

10 *Silver Streak*, directed by Arthur Hiller

11 *Silverado*

12 An otter

13 *Never So Few*. The movie was directed by John Sturges

14 *The Little Vampire*

15 *Meetings with Remarkable Men*

Yakima Canutt was the doyen of American stunt men. In *Stage Coach* (1939) he was an Indian jumping on the horses to stop the stage coach. Then he was shot by John Wayne and fell through the horses. When John Wayne jumped on the horses to control them, it was Yakima Canutt again, dressed as the Duke.

Take 13

1   Can you name the 1964 movie in which a US bomber is accidently ordered to destroy Moscow?

2   Name David Lynch's first film.

3   Name the 1977 movie in which Richard Burton plays a psychiatrist trying to unlock the deep-rooted problems of a stable boy, based on Peter Shaffer's successful play.

4   What 1966 movie starred Marlon Brando, Jane Fonda, Robert Redford, Angie Dickenson and Robert Duvall?

5   Name the 1969 western starring Elvis Presley.

6   Edith Evans, Ralph Richardson and Susan Hampshire were in what 1969 movie, based on a Charles Dickens novel?

7   Paul Newman, Joanne Woodward, Diahann Carroll, Sidney Poitier and Louis Armstrong starred in what 1961 jazz romance?

8   Hayley Mills played twins in what delightful 1961 Disney movie?

9   Laurence Olivier and Katharine Hepburn teamed up for what romantic comedy in 1975?

10 Pier Paolo Pasolini made *Gospel According to Matthew* (1966). Who did he dedicate the movie to?

11 Ken Russell directed Gabriel Byrne, Natasha Richardson and Julian Sands in what 1986 movie?

12 Robert Altman directed a 2001 movie in which a murder takes place during a weekend at an English country estate. Name the movie.

13 Name the 1971 movie in which an eccentric thinks he is the real Sherlock Holmes, starring George C. Scott and Joanne Woodward.

14 What Irish actor starred in *The Adventures of Robinson Crusoe* (1954)?

15 Robert Mitchum, Peter Falk, Robert Ryan and Earl Holliman starred in what World War II movie from 1968?

Answers

1   *Fail Safe*. The movie was directed by Sidney Lumet and starred Henry Fonda, Walter Matthau and Larry Hagman

2   *Eraserhead* (1978)

3   *Equus*. The movie also starred Peter Firth, Colin Blakely, Joan Plowright and Jenny Agutter

4   *The Chase*, directed by Arthur Penn

5   *Charro*

6   *David Copperfield*

7   *Paris Blues*

8   *The Parent Trap*. The movie also starred Maureen O'Hara and Brian Keith

9   *Love Among the Ruins*, directed by George Cukor

10 Pope John XXIII

11 *Gothic*

12 *Gosford Park*. The cast included Alan Bates, Charles Dance, Maggie Smith and Stephen Fry

13 *They Might Be Giants*

14 Dan O'Herlihy

15 *Anzio*. The movie also starred Arthur Kennedy

'Failure has a thousand explanations. Success doesn't need one.'
– *Alec Guinness*

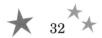

Take 14

1   What was the 1987 movie about shell-shocked survivors of World War I, starring Colin Firth and Kenneth Branagh?

2   Who played Bulldog Drummond in the 1966 thriller *Deadlier Than the Male*?

3   Queen _____ starred alongside Steve Martin in *Bringing Down the House* (2003)?

4   What 2004 movie became the most commercially successful documentary ever?

5   Where is director Peter Jackson from?

6   When did Christopher Reeve first play Superman?

7   What was the name of Dustin Hoffman's character in *Midnight Cowboy* (1969)?

8   What name did Walt Disney originally plan for Mickey Mouse, before his wife persuaded him to name the mouse Mickey?

9   Who starred as the bored housewife who worked in a brothel just for kicks in the movie *Belle de Jour* (1967)?

10   Who directed John Cusack and Ray Liotta in *Identity* (2003)?

11   Who starred with Jackie Chan in *Shanghai Noon* (2000) and *Shanghai Knights* (2002)?

12   James Spader and Maggie Gyllenhall starred in what 2001 provocative dark comedy?

13   Who played Veronica Guerin in Joel Schumacher's 2003 film about the murdered Irish journalist?

14   Who directed *Cold Mountain* (2003), starring Nicole Kidman, Renée Zellwegger and Jude Law?

15   Who played King Arthur in *Monty Python and the Holy Grail* (1975)?

'Awards? Who needs awards? Best fascist director – Adolf Hitler.'
– Woody Allen

Answers

1 *A Month in the Country*

2 Richard Johnson

3 Queen Latifah

4 *Fahernheit 9/11*, directed by Michael Moore

5 New Zealand

6 1978

7 Ratso Rizzo. The movie also starred Jon Voight

8 Mortimer

9 Catherine Deneuve

10 James Mangold

11 Owen Wilson

12 *Secretary*

13 Cate Blanchett

14. Anthony Minghella

15 Graham Chapman

'I've committed the unpardonable sin in Hollywood. I grew up.'
– Nelson Eddy

Take 15

1   Who played Johnny English in the 2003 film of the same name, based on a character from a TV commercial?

2   Who starred opposite Jennifer Lopez in *Maid in Manhattan* (2002)?

3   Who played Leonardo DiCaprio's father in Spielberg's *Catch Me If You Can* (2003)?

4   Who played the ringmaster/werewolf in Tim Burton's *Big Fish* (2003)?

5   Who starred as the female lead in *Underworld* (2003)?

6   *Ripley's Game* (2003) was the sequel to what Jude Law/Matt Damon film of 2000?

7   Can you name the crime thriller from 1975, starring Kurt Russell as a journalist?

8   Charles Laughton and John Mills starred in what comedy from 1953?

9   Who directed Gene Hackman in *The Conversation* (1974)?

10   Who directed *Mystic River* (2003)?

11   Who played 'the three kings' in the 2000 film of the same name?

12   Who played the boxer Rubin 'Hurricane' Carter in the movie *The Hurricane* (1999)?

13   Who played Mister Moses in the 1965 movie of the same name?

14   A giant wild pig with a taste for human flesh terrorised the Australian outback in what 1984 movie?

15   Who played the Boston Strangler in the movie of the same name from 1968?

'Everything you hear about Hollywood is true – including the lies.'
– Orson Welles

Answers

1. Rowan Atkinson
2. Ralph Fiennes
3. Christopher Walken
4. Danny DeVito
5. Kate Beckinsale
6. *The Talented Mr. Ripley*
7. *The Mean Season*
8. *Hobson's Choice*
9. Francis Ford Coppola
10. Clint Eastwood
11. George Clooney, Mark Whalberg and Ice Cube
12. Denzel Washington
13. Robert Mitchum. The movie starred Carroll Baker
14. *Razorback*
15. Tony Curtis

'Good original screenplays are almost as rare in Hollywood as virgins.'
– *Raymond Chandler*

Take 16

1. What murdered rap artist starred in the 1994 basketball movie *Above the Rim*?
2. Clint Eastwood and Gene Hackman starred in what political thriller of 1996?
3. Ed Harris and Michael Biehn played the male leads in *Abyss* (1989), directed by James Cameron. Who played the female lead?
4. Who directed Dustin Hoffman in *Accidental Hero* (1992)?
5. In the controversial film *The Accused* (1988), who won her first Oscar as the lead character?
6. Who starred in *Ace Ventura: Pet Detective* (1994)?
7. Who wrote the dark cult drama *The Acid House* (1998)?
8. Who starred in the tough drama *Act of Vengeance* (1986)?
9. Dennis Hopper starred as a shy, unhappily married pipe smoker in what 1995 film?
10. Who directed *The Addams Family* (1991)?
11. Name the male and female leads in Abel Ferrara's *The Addiction* (1994).
12. In what 1989 Terry Gilliam film did John Neville, Eric Idle, Oliver Reed and Uma Thurman appear?
13. Name the 1965 survival adventure movie, set in South Africa, starring Stuart Whitman, Stanley Baker and Susannah York.
14. *The Bachelor* (1999), starring Chris O'Donnell, was a remake of what 1925 Buster Keaton classic?
15. Who directed *For the Love of the Game* (1999), starring Kevin Costner?

'I can't play a loser. I don't look like one.'
– *Rock Hudson*

Answers

1   Tupac Shakur, who died on Friday 13 September 1995
2   *Absolute Power*, directed by Clint Eastwood
3   Mary Elisabeth Mastrantonio
4   Stephen Frears
5   Jodie Foster. She won her second Oscar for *Silence of the Lambs* (1991)
6   Jim Carrey
7   Irvine Welsh, who was also responsible for *Trainspotting*
8   Charles Bronson
9   *Acts of Love*
10 Barry Sonnenfeld, whose most profitable work has been the *Men in Black* series
11 Christopher Walken and Lili Taylor. This film features a host of *Soprano* stars
12 *The Adventures of Baron Munchausen*. The film flopped in the box office but redeemed itself from video and DVD sales
13 *Sands of the Kalahari*, directed by Cy Enfield
14 *Seven Chances*
15 Sam Raimi. He followed this movie up with *Spider-Man* (2002)

'Always cast against the part and it won't be boring.'
– *David Lean*

Take 17

1   In what year was the Oscar-winning movie *Rocky*, starring Sylvester Stallone, released?

2   Who gave voice to the wise cracking baby Mikey in *Look Who's Talking* (1989)?

3   Veteran Bond director John Glen directed *For Your Eyes Only* (1981). What number film was this in the 007 franchise?

4   Elizabeth Taylor and Richard Burton starred in what 1967 movie set in Haiti and based on a Graham Greene Novel?

5   Who starred as Stephen Price in the 1999 version of *House on Haunted Hill*?

6   Who plays Vinny in *My Cousin Vinny* (1992)?

7   Who starred in the action adventure movie *Nowhere To Run* (1992)?

8   The son of which famous British director made *Plunkett and Macleane* (1999)?

9   Who played the character Martin Cahill in *Ordinary Decent Criminal* (1999)?

10 Akira Kurosawa's *Rashomon* (1950) was remade in 1964 and starred Paul Newman. Can you name the remake?

11 Who plays the male lead in *Patch Adams* (1998)?

12 Name the 1991 movie by Ken Loach which gave Robert Carlyle his first shot at stardom.

13 Who directed Nick Nolte in the thought-provoking *Q&A* (1990)?

14 Who played Oskar Schindler in *Schindlers List* (1993)?

15 Who led the cast of John Dahl's *Red Rock West* (1992)?

'Stars are people who sell a lot of popcorn.'
– *Harrison Ford*

Answers

1   1976. It won Best Picture and Best Actor for Sly Stallone

2   Bruce Willis

3   It was the twelfth Bond film and starred Roger Moore as 007

4   The Comedians. The movie also starred Alec Guinness, Peter Ustinov and Lillian Gish

5   Geoffrey Rush

6   Joe Pesci

7   Jean Claude Van Damme

8   Jake Scott, son of Ridley

9   Kevin Spacey

10   *The Outrage*

11   Robin Williams

12   *Riff-Raff.* The movie also starred Ricky Tomlinson

13   Sidney Lumet

14   Liam Neeson

15   Nicolas Cage

'I am careful not to confuse excellence with perfection.
Excellence I can reach for; perfection is God's business.'
– Michael J. Fox

Take 18

1   Who played the male lead in the football comedy *Fever Pitch* (1996)?

2   Who directed Tom Cruise, Demi Moore And Jack Nicholson in *A Few Good Men* (1992)?

3   Who played Larry Flynt in *The People Vs Larry Flynt* (1996)?

4   *X-files* veteran director James Wong made his feature debut with what 2000 film starring Devon Sava and Sean William Scott?

5   Name the two leads in *Rain Man* (1988), directed by Barry Levinson.

6   Walter Matthau directed and starred in what crime drama from 1959?

7   Which stand-up comedian made a film called *Live on the Sunset Strip* (1982)?

8   What was Bruce Lee's final film?

9   Who played Private Ryan in Spielberg's *Saving Private Ryan* (1998)?

10   Who directed *Indian in the Cupboard* (1995)?

11   Directed by Danny Boyle and starring Ewan McGregor, name this 1994 black comedy.

12   Who directed *Jade* (1995) starring David Caruso and Chazz Palminteri?

13   What 1939 film did Orson Welles watch forty times in preparation for directing *Citizen Kane* (1941)?

14   Who played the love interest of Hawkeye in Michael Mann's 1992 remake of *The Last of the Mohicans*?

15   Corey Haim played a disabled kid and Gary Busey played his drunken uncle. Name the 2002 werewolf horror movie from a short story by Stephen King.

'Hollywood didn't kill Marilyn Monroe. It's the Marilyn Monroes
who are killing Hollywood.'
– *Billy Wilder*

Answers

1   Colin Firth

2   Rob Reiner

3   Woody Harrelson. The movie, directed by Milos Foreman, also starred Courtney Love and Edward Norton

4   *Final Destination*

5   Dustin Hoffman and Tom Cruise

6   *Gangster Story*

7   Richard Pryor

8   *Game of Death* (1978)

9   Matt Damon

10   Frank Oz

11   *Shallow Grave*

12   William Friedkin

13   *Stagecoach*. The movie starred John Wayne and was directed by John Ford

14   Madeline Stowe

15   *Silver Bullet*

'I have the most wonderful memory for forgetting things.'
– Marilyn Monroe

Take 19

1   Name the lead actors in John Woo's *Face / Off* (1997).

2   Can you name Matt Dillon's first film?

3   What did Orson Welles promise not to do for one hour in his excellent documentary-style film *F for Fake* (1973)?

4   In what 1983 film did Tom Cruise, Patrick Swayze, Matt Dillon and Emilio Estevez appear?

5   What 1993 film teamed Clint Eastwood and Kevin Costner together?

6   Who directed Harrison Ford in the 1996 version of *Sabrina*?

7   Who starred as Santa in *The Santa Clause* (1994)?

8   Who starred as real-life cop Frank Serpico in Sidney Lumet's *Serpico* (1973)?

9   Who directed *A Simple Plan* (1998) starring Bill Paxton, Billy Bob Thornton and Bridget Fonda?

10 In *Wargames* (1983), who played the teenage computer nerd who hacked into the US government's defence system and virtually started a nuclear war?

11 What 2000 film dealt with secret societies and starred TV's *Dawson's Creek* celebrity Joshua Jackson?

12 Which *Matrix* star appeared in all these films from 1986: *Act of Vengeance*, *Babes in Toyland*, *Brotherhood of Justice*, *Under the Influence* and *Young Again*?

13 What are the only words Hulk utters in Ang Lee's 2003 big screen version of *Hulk*?

14 Name the 1992 movie starring Al Pacino, Jack Lemmon and Kevin Spacey.

15 Who directed *Lost in Translation* (2003), starring Bill Murray and Scarlett Johannson?

Syria banned the movie *Giant* (1956) because Elizabeth Taylor
was a supporter of the Israeli state.

# Answers

1   Nicolas Cage and John Travolta
2   *Over the Edge* (1979)
3   He promised not to lie in his film about the deception of reality
4   *The Outsiders*, directed by Francis Ford Coppola
5   *A Perfect World*, directed by Clint Eastwood
6   Sydney Pollack
7   Tim Allen
8   Al Pacino
9   Sam Raimi
10   Matthew Broderick
11   *The Skulls*
12   Keanu Reeves
13   'Puny Human'
14   Glengarry Glenross
15   Sofia Coppola

'Bob Hope is not a comedian. He just translates what others write for him.'
– *Groucho Marx*

Take 20

1   This 1970 Oscar-winning documentary highlighted the tensions that would inevitably lead to the demise of the Beatles. Name the movie.

2   Complete the film title: Jason and_____ _____ (1963).

3   Who starred in *Behold a Pale Horse* (1964)?

4   *Master and Commander: The Far Side of the World* (2003), starring Russell Crowe, was set during which wars?

5   Laurence Harvey starred as a talent agent trying to sign up Cliff Richard in what 1959 movie?

6   What 1955 Victorian melodrama starred Stewart Granger and Jean Simmons?

7   Curtis Hanson (*LA Confidential*, 1998) directed Tom Cruise in what 1983 movie?

8   Who played Dr. Ian Malcolm in Steven Spielberg's *Jurassic Park* (1993)?

9   Name the two male leads in *Just Cause* (1995)?

10 Which *Soprano* star appears alongside Demi Moore in *The Juror* (1996)?

11 Roger Avary, director of *Killing Zoe* (1993), co-wrote which 1994 Tarantino movie?

12 Who played Mathilda in Luc Besson's *Leon* (1994)?

13 Who played Roger Murtaugh in the *Lethal Weapon* films?

14 Name the Coreys who starred in the caper *License To Drive* (1998)?

15 Who played the lead in *Three Colours Blue* (1993)?

'Over the past 50 years Bob Hope employed 88 joke writers . . . who supplied him with more than one million jokes. And he still couldn't make me laugh.'
– *Eddie Murphy*

Answers

1   *Let It Be*

2   *Jason and the Argonauts*

3   Gregory Peck, Anthony Quinn and Omar Sharif

4   The Napoleonic Wars

5   *Expresso Bongo*

6   *Footsteps in the Fog*

7   *Losin' It*

8   Jeff Goldblum. He reprised his role for the 1997 sequel, *Jurassic Park: The Lost World*

9   Sean Connery and Laurence Fishburne

10   James Gandolfini

11   *Pulp Fiction*

12   Natalie Portman. The movie also starred Jean Reno and Gary Oldman

13   Danny Glover

14   Corey Haim and Corey Feldman. Both actors also appeared in Joel Schumaker's *The Lost Boys* (1987)

15   Juliette Binoche. The movie was directed by Krzystof Kieslowski

'Clark Gable is the sort of guy if you say "Hiya Clark, how are yah?",
he's stuck for an answer.'
– *Ava Gardner*

Take 21

1   Name the actor who played Shaft in the original films of the same name?

2   Michael Mann's *Heat* (1995) was an extravagant remake of an earlier film he also directed. Name it.

3   Russell Crowe played a whistle blower in what 1999 Michael Mann film?

4   Which rock musician appeared in *Fight Club* (1999), directed by David Fincher?

5   Name the director of *Lock, Stock and Two Smoking Barrels* (1998) and *Snatch* (2000)?

6   John Carpenter directs, produces and writes his films. What else does he contribute?

7   What actor played a masked villain in *Panic Room* (2002) and is also an American country singer?

8   From what book does the film *Ghost Dog* (2001) draw its influence?

9   What characters did Mike Myers play in the *Austin Powers* movies?

10   Which composer's score was so good for the original film *Cape Fear* (1962) that Martin Scorcese used it in his 1991 remake of the same name?

11   Who directed *The Shawshank Redemption* (1994), starring Tim Robbins and Morgan Freeman? Name the other epic prison movie he also directed.

12   Which famous director was a classmate of composer Ennio Morricone?

13   Name the character that Oscar winner Daniel Day Lewis portrayed in Martin Scorcese's epic *Gangs of New York* (2001)?

14   Who played the 'Headless Horseman' in Tim Burton's *Sleepy Hollow* (1999)?

15   Who played Beethoven in *Immortal Beloved* (1994)?

Answers

1. Richard Roundtree. He also played a cameo part in the reworking of *Shaft* (2000), starring Samuel L. Jackson.
2. *LA Takedown*
3. *The Insider*. This film was based on real events and made a good case for anti-smoking
4. Meatloaf Aday. He appeared as an overweight 'juicer' who had grown breasts because of misuse of steroids
5. Guy Ritchie
6. He also scores the music for his films
7. Dwight Yoakum
8. *Hagakure (In the Shadow of the Leaves): The Book of the Samurai*
9. He played Austin Powers, Dr. Evil, Fat Bastard and Goldmember
10. Bernard Herrmann's memorable score was rearranged by Elmer Bernstein
11. Frank Darabont. He also directed Tom Hanks in *The Green Mile* (1999)
12. Sergio Leone
13. Bill the Butcher
14. Christopher Walken
15. Gary Oldman

'I suggest we hire a telephone box and invite all his friends to the party.'
– Doug Hayward (on Rex Harrison's 70th birthday)

Take 22

1 Who starred in Stanley Kubrick's *Paths of Glory* (1957)?

2 Name the two stars of *Bus Stop* (1956)?

3 Who played Grey Owl in Richard Attenborough's 1999 movie of the same name?

4 Who played the leading role in the movie *The Spy Who Came in from the Cold* (1965)?

5 Malcolm McDowell starred in what 1968 drama about public school life, directed by Lindsay Anderson?

6 Tim Robbins played a top Hollywood executive in what 1992 movie?

7 Name the two movies about Christopher Columbus, both released in 1992.

8 Susan Sarandon, Nick Nolte and Peter Ustinov starred in what 1992 drama based on a true story?

9 Name the two actors who played the Washington reporters Bob Woodward and Carl Bernstein in *All the President's Men* (1976).

10 Who played Billy Holliday in *Lady Sings the Blues* (1972)?

11. Name the two lovers in *Love Story* (1970).

12 What 1993 movie starred Mel Gibson and was also his directorial debut?

13 Who played Napoleon Solo and Illya Kuryakin in both *The Man from U.N.C.L.E.* TV series and the movie spin-offs?

14 He played 'the pawnbroker' in the 1965 movie of the same title. Can you name the actor?

15 Glenn Ford, Shirley MacLaine and Leslie Nielsen starred in what 1958 comedy western?

'Clark has a magnificent set of dazzling teeth –
they were made by a dentist named Wallace.'
– *Lilli Palmer (on Clark Gable)*

Answers

1. Kirk Douglas
2. Marilyn Monroe and Don Murray
3. Pierce Brosnan
4. Richard Burton
5. *If . . .*
6. *The Player*, directed by Robert Altman
7. *Christopher Columbus: The Discovery* and *1492: The Conquest of Paradise*
8. *Lorenzo's Oil*
9. Robert Redford and Dustin Hoffman
10. Diana Ross
11. Ryan O'Neal and Ali McGraw
12. *The Man Without a Face*
13. Robert Vaughn and David McCallum
14. Rod Steiger
15. *The Sheepman*

'King of Hollywood? If Clark Gable had an inch less he'd be called "Queen of Hollywood".'
– *Carole Lombard (on her husband)*

Take 23

1   How much money was Arnold Schwarzenegger paid to reprise his role as the Terminator in *Terminator 3: The Rise of the Machines*?

2   Name the love interest of Bruce Banner in Ang Lee's *Hulk* (2001).

3   Kate Hudson starred in *Almost Famous* (2000) directed by Cameron Crowe. Which famous female actor is she daughter of?

4   Who played the female lead in *Erin Brockovich* (2000)?

5   Finish Edward Norton's line in Spike Lee's *25th Hour* (2002): 'Champagne for my real friends _____.'

6   Can you name the Oscar-winning actor in Roman Polanski's *The Pianist* (2002)?

7   The US production of *The Ring* (2002) is a remake of an original movie *The Ring* (1997). From what country did the earlier film originate?

8   Gary Cooper and Ingrid Bergman starred in what 1943 war drama based on Ernest Hemmingway's classic novel?

9   Name the 1992 horror movie set in Afica, about a serial killer who was a hitcher.

10.   Adam Sandler and Emily Watson starred in what 2002 P.T. Anderson picture?

11   Who played the lead in Cyrano de Bergerac (1990)?

12   David Fincher directed Brad Pitt in two films, what were they?

13   *Harry Potter and the Philosopher's Stone* (2001) was renamed for the American audience. What was its new title?

14   Name the two films in which Al Pacino and Robert De Niro appeared together.

15   *Orlando* (1992), starring Tilda Swinton, was an adaptation of whose novel?

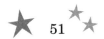

Answers

1. He was paid a staggering $50 million
2. Jennifer Connelly
3. Goldie Hawn
4. Julia Roberts
5. '. . . real pain for my sham friends.'
6. Adrien Brody
7. Japan. There have been sequels but none matched the terror of the original Japanese version
8. *For Whom the Bell Tolls*
9. *Dust Devil*
10. *Punch Drunk Love* (2002)
11. Gerard Depardieu
12. *Se7en* (1995) and *Fight Club* (1999). Both films have excellent twists
13. *Harry Potter and the Sorcerer's Stone*
14. *Heat* (1995) and *Godfather Part II* (1974), although they don't actually share any screen time together in the latter
15. Virginia Woolf. Quentin Crisp played Elizabeth I

A cinema manager was arrested in 1967 in High Point USA for showing a movie called *Hawaii* (1966). It showed bare breasted natives and starred Julie Andrews.

Take 24

1   Which *Lord of the Rings* star made a brief appearance in *Back to the Future 2* (1989)?

2   Which Asian star was thrown out of a window in Bruce Lee's *Fist of Fury* (1972) and had his neck broken in *Enter the Dragon* (1973)?

3   What wrestler starred in John Carpenter's *They Live* (1988)?

4   Rome was the setting for a romantic liaison between Gregory Peck and Audrey Hepburn what 1953 movie?

5   In the fantasy adventure *The Three Worlds of Gulliver* (1959), who played Dr Lemuel Gulliver?

6   Spencer Tracy and Robert Ryan starred in what modern western from 1955, directed by John Sturges?

7   Which tough action star lent his voice talents to the animated film *The Iron Giant* (1999)?

8   Jessica Lange played country singer Patsy Cline in what 1985 biopic?

9   Eric Bana starred in *Chopper* (2000) and *Black Hawk Down (2002)*. What *Marvel* comic character did he portray more recently?

10 What was the name of Sergio Leone's final film?

11 Football stars Bobby Moore and Pelé appeared in what 1981 World War II movie?

12 Which two male actors starred in the recent remake of Graham Greene's *The Quiet American (2002)*?

13 Who played the lead role in the epic fantasy movie *Conan the Barbarian* (1983)?

14 Who wrote the screenplay for the 1983 remake of the gangster epic *Scarface,* starring Al Pacino?

15 Michael J. Fox was the mouse and Nathan Lane was the cat in this fantasy, which also starred Hugh Laurie and Geena Davis. Name the movie.

Answers

1 Elijah Wood

2 Jackie Chan

3 'Rowdy' Roddy Piper

4 *Roman Holiday*. Jean Simmons was the first choice for the role of
   Princess Anne

5 Kerwin Matthews

6 *Bad Day at Blackrock*

7 Vin Diesel

8 *Sweet Dreams*. Ed Harris co-starred.

9 The Hulk

10 *Once Upon a Time in America* (1984)

11 *Escape to Victory*. The movie also starred Sylvester Stallone and
    Michael Caine

12 Michael Caine and Brendan Fraser

13 Arnold Schwarzenegger

14 Oliver Stone

15 *Stuart Little*

'Arnold Schwarzenegger is not an actor, he's a special effect.'
– John Millius

Take 25

1   Jack Nicholson appeared alongside which actor in *One Flew Over the Cuckoo's Nest* (1975) and *Hoffa* (1992)?

2   What fast-talking comedian starred with Jackie Chan in the *Rush Hour* films?

3   What hip-hop artist scored the music for *Ghost Dog* (2000) and the recent *Kill Bill* movies?

4   Paul Newman and Robert Redford appeared in two George Roy Hill Oscar-winning films. Can you name them?

5   In what 2001 film was the main character haunted by a time-travelling rabbit named Frank?

6   Dirk Bogarde and Silviana Mangano acted together in what drama from 1971, directed by Luchino Visconti?

7   What child actor had a small role as Tim Robbins' son in *Jacob's Ladder* (1990)?

8   Emilio Estevez is the son of which famous actor?

9   Which Irish beach was used to film the opening sequence in *Saving Private Ryan* (1998)?

10 Quentin Tarantino resurrected the ailing career of which former Hollywood heart-throb and in what 1994 film?

11 Which handsome British actor played the main role in *Existenz* (1999)?

12 What is the name of Johnny Depp's character in *Pirates of the Caribbean* (2003)?

13 Which Irish musician starred in Pink Floyd's film *The Wall* (1982)?

14 Brandon Lee, son of Bruce, tragically died during the production of which 1994 film?

15 Which famous couple, now divorced, appeared as husband and wife in Stanley Kubrick's final film *Eyes Wide Shut* (1999)?

Answers

1 Danny De Vito. De Vito also directed *Hoffa* (1992), a portrayal of the infamous Union Leader of America

2 Chris Tucker, who began his career as a stand-up comedian

3 The RZA, leading rapper and producer of the Wu-Tang Clan

4 *Butch Cassidy and the Sundance Kid* (1969) and *The Sting* (1973)

5 *Donnie Darko*, made by first-time director Richard Kelly for under $5m

6 *Death in Venice*

7 Macauley Culkin, better known as the kid from *Home Alone* (1990)

8 Martin Sheen. Estevez is also a brother to Charlie Sheen

9 Ballinesker/Curracloe beach in Co. Wexford

10 John Travolta, in *Pulp Fiction*

11 Jude Law

12 Jack Sparrow. Johnny Depp supposedly modelled his character on the behaviour of the Rolling Stones band member Keith Richards

13 Bob Geldolf

14 *The Crow.* Lee was shot at point blank range. The gun was loaded with live ammunition when it should have being carrying blanks

15 Tom Cruise and Nicole Kidman

'My advice to widows – don't sell your house and don't sleep with Frank Sinatra.'
– Lauren Bacall

Take 26

1   What was Seabiscuit in the 2003 movie of the same name and based on Laura Hillenbrand's bestselling book?

2   Who played the leading role in *Tears of the Sun* (2003), set in war-torn Nigeria?

3   Which veteran British actor starred as Harold Smith in *Whatever Happened to Harold Smith?* (1999)?

4   Who directed *Space Cowboys* (2000)?

5   Who was the leading star in *Space Jam* (1997)?

6   Who plays the President of the USA in *Deep Impact* (1998), directed by Mimi Leder?

7   *Cruel Intentions* (1999) starring Sarah Michelle Gellar, Ryan Phillipe and Reese Witherspoon is a remake of what 1988 film?

8   In what 2002 off-beat drama do Samuel L. Jackson and Ben Affleck star opposite each other?

9   Mickey Rourke and Tupac Shakur star in what 1995 gangster cop movie?

10 What type of virus struck down the five college friends in *Cabin Fever* (2002)?

11 Horror comedy *The Dentist* (1999) was directed by Brian Yuzna. What zombie horror film is Brian Yuzna best known for producing?

12 Name the three male leads in *Fallen* (1998).

13 Cate Blanchett, Minnie Driver, Rupert Everett and Julianne Moore starred in what 1999 comedy, based on an Oscar Wilde stage play?

14 Which government department openly criticised the movie *Heartbreak Ridge* (1986) and why?

15 Who played the gangster's chauffeur in the crime thriller Mona Lisa (1986)?

'I always knew Frank would end up in bed with a boy.'
– *Ava Gardner (on Mia Farrow)*

Answers

1   A racehorse. The movie starred Tobey Maguire and Jeff Bridges

2   Bruce Willis

3   Tom Courtenay

4   Clint Eastwood

5   Michael Jordan

6   Morgan Freeman, also starring Robert Duvall, Tea Leoni and Elijah Wood

7   *Dangerous Liaisons*

8   *Changing Lanes*, directed by Roger Michell

9   *Bullet*

10 A flesh-eating virus

11 *Re-Animator*

12 Denzel Washington, John Goodman and Donald Sutherland

13 *An Ideal Husband*

14 The US Department of Defense. They said: 'Drill sergeants are not permitted by regulations to swear at recruits.'

15 Bob Hoskins. The movie was directed by Neil Jordan

'Hanging around with Sinatra was like walking in a minefield.'
– Dean Martin

Take 27

1. Name the elegant 2000 martial arts movie, from director Ang Lee, set in China and telling the tale of a stolen antique sword.

2. Name the 1972 rite-of-passage western about a boy's journey into manhood in the wake of the American Civil War.

3. Audrey Hepburn's final movie was directed by Steven Spielberg and also starred Richard Dreyfuss, Holly Hunter and John Goodman. Name this 1989 movie.

4. Name the 1994 erotic thriller starring Bill Pullman and Linda Fiorentino.

5. Who directed *Midnight in the Garden of Good and Evil* (1998), based on John Berendit's bestseller?

6. What trio starred in *Rosencrantz and Guildenstern Are Dead* (1990), based on a Tom Stoppard play?

7. Drew Barrymore starred in the story of Cinderella. Name the 1998 movie.

8. What 2000 movie was based on comedian Brendan O'Carroll's bestselling book *The Mammy*?

9. What 1999 movie was based on a Graham Greene novel and starred Ralph Fiennes and Julianne Moore?

10. Name the 1981 drama starring Jack Lemmon and Sissy Spacek, set in Chile in 1973.

11. Who directed the musical drama *Fame* (1980)?

12. Keanu Reeves, Cameron Diaz and Dan Akroyd starred in what low budget quirky comedy drama of 1996?

13. Michael Palin, Maggie Smith and Trevor Howard starred in what 1982 comedy?

14. Who played the mad scientist in *Gremlins 2: The New Batch* (1990)?

15. Who made his directorial debut with the film *Harlem Nights* (1989), starring Eddie Murphy and Richard Pryor?

Answers

1. *Crouching Tiger, Hidden Dragon*
2. *The Culpepper Cattle Company*, starring Gary Grimes and Billy Green Bush
3. *Always*
4. *The Last Seduction*
5. Clint Eastwood. The movie starred Kevin Spacey and John Cusack
6. Gary Oldman, Tim Roth and Richard Dreyfuss
7. *Ever After*
8. *Agnes Browne*, starring Angelica Huston and Ray Winstone
9. *End of the Affair*, directed by Neil Jordan
10. *Missing*
11. Alan Parker
12. *Feeling Minnesota*
13. *The Missionary*
14. Christopher Lee
15. Eddie Murphy

The first child star to earn over $2 million was Jackie Coogan who starred in such films as *The Kid* (1921). He received $6 per week pocket money.

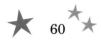

Take 28

1   Martin Brest directed Robert De Niro in what 1988 comedy thriller?

2   This prison drama from 1998, set in Malaysia, starred Vince Vaughn, Anne Heche and Joaquin Phoenix. Name the movie.

3   Who played the wacky father in the film *Moving* (1988)?

4   Jeremy Irons won an Oscar for his performance in this movie from 1990. Can you name it?

5   Who played Jason Patric's father in John Boorman's thriller *Incognito* (1997)?

6   What was the name of the 2000 sequel to the *Blair Witch Project* (1999)?

7   Who played the beautiful Marcia Brady in *The Brady Bunch Movie* (1995)?

8   Who starred in the World War II comedy *The Pigeon that Took Rome* (1962)?

9   What was the name of Mel Gibson's character in the Oscar-winning *Braveheart* (1995)?

10 Name Ang Lee's 1999 film about the American Civil War, starring Skeet Ulrich, Tobey Maguire and Jewel.

11 Who directed Jim Carrey and Matthew Broderick in *Cable Guy* (1996)?

12 Robert Duvall wrote, produced, directed and starred in what movie from 1997 about a Pentecostal preacher?

13 Who played the twin brothers in David Cronenberg's *Dead Ringers* (1988)?

14 Who starred with Mark Wahlberg in *The Corrupter* (1999)?

15 Curtis Hanson directed, Meryl Streep starred, and Kevin Bacon and John C. Reilly played the armed robbers. Can you name this white water rafting thriller from 1994?

'To know Barbra is not necessarily to love her.'
– *Rex Reed (on Barbra Streisand)*

Answers

1   *Midnight Run.* The movie also starred Charles Grodin

2   *Return to Paradise*

3   Richard Pryor

4   *Reversal of Fortune.* The movie also starred Glenn Close and Annabella Sciorra

5   Rod Steiger

6   *Book of Shadows: Blair Witch 2*

7   Christine Taylor

8   Charlton Heston and Elsa Martinelli

9   William Wallace. The movie also starred Sophie Marceau, Patrick McGoohan and Brendan Gleeson, and was directed by Mel Gibson

10   *Ride With the Devil*

11   Ben Stiller

12   *The Apostle*

13   Jeremy Irons

14   Chow Yun Fat

15   *The River Wild*

'If Streisand collided with a mac truck, it's the truck that would drop dead.
(Who ever heard of a truck dropping dead?)'
– John Simon

Take 29

1. Who was the male lead in *The Shipping News* (2001)?

2. In *Glengarry Glen Ross* (1992), about struggling salesmen starring Al Pacino and Jack Lemmon, what did ABC stand for?

3. Who played Halle Berry's husband stranded on death row in *Monster's Ball* (2001)?

4. Who were the male leads in *Rising Sun* (1993)?

5. Who played the parish priest in *Ryan's Daughter* (1970)?

6. Name the British actor who played the villain in *Thunderbirds* (2004), a live action version of the TV series?

7. Who played Catwoman in the 2004 movie of the same name?

8. Who directed *The Grinch* (2000), starring Jim Carrey as Dr. Seuess's most famous character?

9. Who played the female lead in *Freaky Friday* (2003)?

10. Gary Cooper and Lilli Palmer starred in what Fritz Lang classic from 1946?

11. Name the 2000 movie starring Dennis Quaid and Jim Caviezel, in which a son can communicate with his father on an old ham radio.

12. What type of mammal was featured in *Free Willy* (1993)?

13. Mel Gibson's company produced a movie in 1997 with Peter O'Toole and Harvey Keitel, and a cameo by Mel Gibson. Can you name the movie?

14. Name the 1975 movie, directed by John Schlesinger, about Hollywood losers, and starring Donald Sutherland.

15. What was the British movie from 1961 which starred a young Sean Connery and a sinister Herbert Lom?

'There but for the grace of God, goes God.'
– *Herman Mankiewicz (on Orson Welles)*

Answers

1   Kevin Spacey

2   Always Be Closing. The movie also starred Ed Harris, Alan Arkin, Alec Baldwin and Jonathon Pryce

3   Sean (P. Diddy) Combs. The movie also starred Billy Bob Thornton and Heath Ledger

4   Sean Connery and Wesley Snipes

5   Trevor Howard

6   Ben Kingsley

7   Halle Berry

8   Ron Howard

9   Jamie Lee Curtis

10   *Cloak and Dagger*

11   *Frequency*

12   An orca (killer whale). There were two sequels, in 1995 and 1997

13   *Fairy Tale: A True Story*

14   *The Day of the Locust*

15   *The Frightened City*

'Stardom? I never touch the stuff.'
– *John Lithgow*

Take 30

1   Peter O'Toole played a self-styled God in what movie of 1972?

2   Jon Voight played a hardened convict in what 1985 movie?

3   Who played Cromwell in the 1970 movie of the same title?

4   Directed by Luchino Visconti and starring Helmut Berger as a mad king, what was this 1973 movie?

5   In what 1983 movie did Oprah Winfrey star, alongside Whoopi Goldberg?

6   What was Rock Hudson's profession in the comedy film *Pillow Talk* (1960)?

7   Name the two male leads in *My Beautiful Laundrette* (1985)?

8   Who starred in *American Splendor* (2003)?

9   Who directed *Ghosts of Mars* (2001), starring Natasha Henstridge and Ice Cube?

10 Name the two male leads in *Arlington Road* (1998)?

11 James Coburn won a best supporting actor Oscar for what 1998 film?

12 Who starred opposite Will Smith in Barry Sonnenfeld's *Wild Wild West* (1999)?

13 Val Kilmer and Kurt Russell starred in what 1993 western?

14 Who directed *Gallipoli* (1981)?

15 Can you name the black comedy from 1969 starring Oliver Reed, Diana Rigg and Telly Savalas?

'Stars are small people with big heads.'
– *Gore Vidal*

Answers

1 *The Ruling Class.* The movie also starred Alistair Sim, Arthur Lowe and Harry Andrews

2 *Runaway Train.* The movie was based on a screenplay by Akira Kurosawa

3 Richard Harris. The movie also starred Alec Guinness and Robert Morley

4 *Ludwig*

5 *The Color Purple*

6 A songwriter

7 Daniel Day Lewis and Gordon Warnecke

8 Paul Giamatti

9 John Carpenter

10 Jeff Bridges and Tim Robbins

11 *Affliction*

12 Kevin Kline

13 *Tombstone*

14 Peter Weir

15 *The Assassination Bureau*

'Burt and Kirk eat directors for lunch.'
– Shelley Winters (on Burt Lancaster and Kirk Douglas)

Take 31

1   What wrestler-turned-politician appeared alongside Arnie in *Predator* (1987)?

2   Who played 'John Doe' in David Fincher's bleak post-modern film noir classic *Se7en* (1995)?

3   Who wrote the story for *Raiders of the Lost Ark* (1981)?

4   Who starred as Titus Andronicus in the 1999 movie *Titus*?

5   Tom Berenger and Billy Zane starred in what 1992 film set in Panama?

6   Who was originally intended to direct the sci-fi adventure movie *The Philadelphia Experiment* (1984)?

7   Clark Gable and Sophia Loren starred in what movie from 1960?

8   Who narrated *A River Runs Through It* (1992), starring Brad Pitt?

9   What all-American hero wrestler starred in *The Secret Agent Club* (1985)?

10 *The Rainmaker* (1997) is based on whose novel?

11 Name the three leads in *Primary Colours* (1998) directed by Mike Nichols.

12 Kathryn Bigelow directed what 1986 cult vampire movie?

13 Name the male and female leads in *Proof of Life* (2000).

14 Glenn Ford and Bette Davis were cast together in what Frank Capra movie from 1961?

15 Sean Connery and Nicolas Cage teamed up in what Jerry Bruckheimer produced and Michael Bay directed film of 1996?

In *Raiders of the Lost Ark* Indiana Jones has to fight a huge villain with a scimitar.
Harrison Ford at the time was suffering from diarrhoea and didn't feel like
fighting so he suggested to the director, 'why don't I just shoot him?'
He did. And it's one of the funniest scenes in the movie.

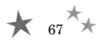

Answers

1. Jesse 'The Body' Ventura. Directed by John McTiernan
2. Kevin Spacey
3. George Lucas
4. Anthony Hopkins
5. *Sniper*
6. John Carpenter. Stewart Raffill took over due to the pre-production limbo of almost ten years
7. *It Started in Naples*
8. It was narrated and directed by Robert Redford
9. Hulk Hogan
10. John Grisham. The movie was directed by Francis Ford Coppola
11. John Travolta, Emma Thompson and Billy Bob Thornton
12. *Near Dark* starring Bill Paxton
13. Russell Crowe and Meg Ryan
14. *A Pocketful of Miracles*
15. *The Rock*

'Until you're known in my profession as a monster, you're not a star.'
– Bette Davis

Take 32

1 Who played the young lead in *Saturday Night and Sunday Morning* (1961)?

2 Name this 1995 psychological drama from cult director Todd Haynes, starring Julianne Moore, about a woman who becomes allergic to 20th century chemical by-products.

3 Which British actor starred in Oliver Stone's *The Hand* (1981)?

4 Who starred in *The Great Imposter* (1961)?

5 What tough guy starred in *Jingle All the Way* (1991)?

6 David Warner and Vanessa Redgrave starred in what 1966 quirky comedy?

7 Which Aussie actor starred in the hard-hitting *Romper Stomper* (1992)?

8 What bawdy comedy from 1969 starred Christopher Plummer and Susannah York?

9 Who directed and starred alongside Charlie Sheen in *The Rookie* (1990)?

10 Cliff Robertson starred in what 1972 western?

11 Who wrote the James Bond theme tune?

12 How many *Halloween* films have there been since the 1978 original starring Jamie Lee Curtis?

13 What do comedy actors Dan Aykroyd, Michael J. Fox and Jim Carrey all have in common?

14 Name Paul Verhoeven's erotic 1995 movie, starring Elizabeth Berkley, Kyle Mac Lachlan and Gina Gershon.

15 What was the first Merchant-Ivory movie from 1985, based on a novel by E.M. Forster, starring Maggie Smith, Helena Bonham Carter and Denholm Elliot?

Answers

1   Albert Finney

2   *Safe*

3   Michael Caine

4   Tony Curtis

5   Arnold Schwarzenegger

6   *Morgan, a Suitable Case for Treatment*

7   Russell Crowe

8   *Lock Up Your Daughters!*

9   Clint Eastwood

10   *The Great Northfield Minnesota Raid*

11   John Barry

12   There have been seven films since the original, which is still perhaps the best and scariest

13   They are all Canadian

14   *Showgirls*

15   *A Room With a View*

'Any star can be devoured by human adoration, sparkle by sparkle.'
– Shirley Temple

Take 33

1   Who played a southern boy expecting to make his fortune as a stud in New York in *Midnight Cowboy* (1969)?

2   What 1969 western musical featured Lee Marvin and Clint Eastwood singing?

3   Who played the Jackal in *The Day of the Jackal* (1973)?

4   What 1982 film featured Eddie Murphy in his first starring role?

5   Who wrote *True Romance* (1993) and who directed it?

6   They say John Cusack put his career on the line to portray a friend of Hitler in what 2002 film?

7   Who played Captain Barbossa in *Pirates of the Caribbean* (2003)?

8   Which country singer starred in the thriller *Higher Ground* (1989)?

9   Who directed and starred in the Italian movie *Life is Beautiful* (1997)?

10 Which brothers directed the period horror *From Hell* (2001), starring Johnny Depp?

11 *Payback* (1998) was a remake of which 1967 John Boorman film that starred Lee Marvin?

12 Melvyn Douglas and Gene Hackman starred in a screen version of Robert Anderson's moving play. Can you name this 1969 movie?

13 Who played Robin Hood in *Time Bandits* (1981)?

14 Name the actor who starred in David Cronenberg's *Videodrome* (1982)?

15 Name the Irish actor who starred in *Tigerland* (2001).

'Life is a long rehearsal for a film that is never made.'
– *Marlene Dietrich*

Answers

1   Jon Voight

2   *Paint Your Wagon*. Lee Marvin's 'Wandering Star' song went to No.1 in the charts.

3   Edward Fox. The movie was directed by Fred Zimmerman

4   *48 Hours*

5   Quentin Tarantino wrote and Tony Scott (brother of Ridley) directed the all-star cast including Christian Slater, Patricia Arquette, Christopher Walken, Brad Pitt and Denis Hopper

6   *Max*. The movie also starred Noah Taylor as a young and 'sensitive' Adolph Hitler

7   Geoffrey Rush

8   John Denver

9   Roberto Benigni

10   The Hughes Brothers (Allen and Albert)

11   *Point Blank*

12   *I Never Sang For My Father*

13   John Cleese

14   James Woods

15   Colin Farrell

'It's very sad. A silver bell has been silenced.'
– George Peppard (on the death of Audrey Hepburn)

Take 34

1   What colour pill did Neo decide to take in *The Matrix* (1999) in order to release his mind and body from the matrix?

2   Name the character played by Sigourney Weaver in the *Alien* films?

3   What was Jack Lemmon's final film appearance in 2000?

4   What sport has featured in more Hollywood movies than any other?

5   Who was originally penned to play the male lead in *Cold Mountain* (2003), but turned it down?

6   Disney released an animation movie in 2003 about an Inuit who turns into an animal. Name the movie.

7   Samuel L. Jackson and Colin Farrell starred together in what thriller from 2003?

8   It was a disappointing remake of a classic horror movie from 1974. Can you name the 2003 movie starring Jessica Biel?

9   Who played Tinkerbell in the 2003 version of *Peter Pan*?

10   A time travel movie from Michael Crichton made in 2003. Can you name it?

11   Who was Tim Burton's first choice for *Edward Scissorhands* (1990)?

12   Who was Rita in *Educating Rita* (1983)?

13   Who starred in the crime thriller *Cop* (1988)?

14   Name the 1978 movie, directed by Terrence Malick, which starred Richard Gere, Brook Adams and Sam Shepard.

15   Name the 1989 movie which was set in apartheid South Africa and starred Donald Sutherland, Janet Suzman and Marlon Brando.

'I won't quit the business until I get run over by a truck,
a producer or a critic.'
– *Jack Lemmon*

Answers

1 Neo took the red pill

2 Ripley. Originally intended to be a male character, but the director, Ridley Scott, thought it would be better played by a female

3 *The Legend of Baggar Vance*, although his name did not appear in the credits

4 Boxing

5 Tom Cruise. Jude Law starred instead

6 *Brother Bear*

7 *S.W.A.T.*

8 *The Texas Chainsaw Massacre*

9 Ludvine Sagnier

10 *Timeline*

11 Tom Cruise. Johnny Depp took over and was perfect as the humanoid

12 Julie Waters

13 James Woods

14 *Days of Heaven*

15 *A Dry White Season*

'When I check into a hotel, I pull out the Gideon bible and rip out the part in Leviticus that says people like me should be removed from the face of the earth.'
– *Sir Ian McKellen*

Take 35

1   What was the first movie made in Hollywood?

2   What actor was the first to get shares in a film's profits?

3   Laurence Olivier and Julie Harris starred in what 1961 movie, set in Mexico?

4   Who starred as Dr. Crippen in the 1964 movie of the same name?

5   Who wrote the novel *Coma* that was made into the 1978 movie of the same name?

6   George Lucas's first film as a director was *THX1138* (1971). Can you name his second movie from 1973?

7   Who played the female lead opposite Dustin Hoffman in *Kramer Vs Kramer* (1979)?

8   A sombre story about poolroom sharks, starring Paul Newman, can you name the 1960 movie?

9   Who starred in *The Jerk* (1980)?

10   Who directed *The Last Movie* (1971)?

11   Which movie producer started his career as an actor, making his debut in *Man of a Thousand Faces* (1957)?

12   Rock Hudson and Julie Andrews starred together in what movie from 1970?

13   Who was the child star in *International Velvet* (1978)

14   Jane Fonda played writer Lillian Hellman in what 1977 movie?

15   Released in 1961, what was Robert Redford's first movie?

'Sometimes I'm not sure there's ever been an America.
I think it's all been Frank Capra's films.'
– John Cassavetes

Answers

1   *The Squaw Man* (1913), directed by Cecil B. DeMille

2   James Stewart in *Winchester '73* (1950)

3   *The Power and the Glory*

4   Donald Pleasence

5   Robin Cook. The movie was directed by Michael Crichton

6   *American Graffiti*

7   Meryl Streep

8   *The Hustler*

9   Steve Martin

10   Dennis Hopper

11   Robert Evans

12   *Darling Lili*, directed by Blake Edwards

13   Tatum O'Neal

14   *Julia*, co-starring Vanessa Redgrave

15   *War Hunt*

The *Our Gang* series, from the early 1930s, was made in English, German,
French and Spanish. The children were taught to speak
the different languages by a coach.

Take 36

1 Name Ang Lee's 1995 romantic period drama, starring Emma Thompson and Kate Winslet.

2 In *On the Waterfront* (1954), who said: 'I coulda been a contender.'?

3 Which martial arts actor is known as 'The muscles from Brussels'?

4 John Wayne's final film with director John Ford was not a western. Name the 1963 movie.

5 Who played the two leads in *Tin Cup* (1996)?

6 James Spader, Andie McDowell and Peter Gallagher starred in this 1989 Palme D'Or winning drama, directed by Steven Soderbergh. Name it.

7 Real-life couple Virginia McKenna and Bill Travers starred as wildlife wardens based in Kenya in what 1966 film?

8 What was Groucho Marx's final film?

9 Name the 1988 movie, directed by Robert Redford, about a New Mexico farmer and water supply.

10 A fishy tale and a pirate story were box office smashes for Disney in 2003. Name the two movies?

11 Who played the evil scanner in *Scanners* (1980)?

12 In which 1953 French movie did Jacques Tati introduce his Monsieur Hulot character?

13 Al Pacino won an Oscar for his performance in what movie from 1992?

14 Who played the heroine in *Pirates of the Caribbean* (2003)?

15 Name the 2002 movie starring Sean Hughes and Richard Attenborough, adapted from Spike Milligan's comic novel.

'My advice to actors – never pass a bathroom.'
– *George Burns*

Answers

1   *Sense and Sensibility*. The movie also starred Alan Rickman and Hugh Grant

2   Marlon Brando

3   Jean-Claude Van Damme

4   *Donovan's Reef*

5   Kevin Costner and Renée Russo

6   *Sex, Lies and Videotape*

7   *Born Free*, directed by James Hill

8   *Skidoo* (1968). The movie also starred Jackie Gleeson

9   *The Milagro Beanfield War*

10 *Finding Nemo* and *Pirates of the Caribbean*

11 Michael Ironside. The movie was directed by David Cronenberg

12 *Monsieur Hulot's Holiday*

13 *Scent of a Woman*, directed by Martin Brest. The movie also starred Chris O'Donnell

14 Keira Knightley

15 *Puckoon*

The most used expression in movie scripts is: 'Let's get outta here.'

Take 37

1 Who played Pontius Pilate in *The Last Temptation of Christ* (1988)?

2 Marlon Brando was directed by Bernardo Bertolucci in what erotic drama from 1972?

3 Dean Martin played a secret agent in *The Silencers* (1966) and *Murderer's Row* (1966). What was the agent's name?

4 Which actor shot to stardom after appearing in Mike Nichol's *The Graduate* (1967)?

5 Who played Rasputin in *Nicholas and Alexandra* (1971)?

6 What was Spencer Tracy's last movie?

7 Glenda Jackson and Peter Finch starred together in what gritty drama from 1971?

8 In Robert Altman's quirky western *McCabe and Mrs Miller* (1971), who played the two leads?

9 What was the 'Poseidon' in the movie *The Poseidon Adventure* (1972)?

10 Who played the young American in Alan Parker's *Midnight Express* (1978)?

11 In *Autumn Sonata* (1978), directed by Ingmar Bergman, who played the two leading roles?

12 In Werner Herzog's *Woyzeck* (1978), who played Woyzeck?

13 Who played Swann in *Swann in Love* (1984)?

14 Who was the male lead in Peter Weir's thriller *Witness* (1985)?

15 In Woody Allen's *The Purple Rose of Cairo* (1985), who played Celia?

'How can anyone be as thin as we can? We have trainers to work us out.
We have specially prepared meals.'
– *Sarah Michelle Gellar (on Hollywood's thin ladies)*

Answers

1   David Bowie

2   *Last Tango in Paris*

3   Matt Helm

4   Dustin Hoffman

5   Tom Baker, who went on to play Dr Who in the TV show of the same name

6   *Guess Who's Coming to Dinner* (1967), with Katharine Hepburn and Sydney Poitier

7   *Sunday Bloody Sunday*

8   Warren Beatty and Julie Christie

9   An ocean liner. The movie starred Gene Hackman, Shelley Winters, Red Buttons and Ernest Borgnine

10 Brad Davis. The movie also starred John Hurt

11 Liv Ullmann and Ingrid Bergman

12 Klaus Kinski

13 Jeremy Irons

14 Harrison Ford

15 Mia Farrow

The Hays Office was founded in 1922 to regulate the motion picture industry.
The president was postmaster general Will H. Hayes. After silent film star
Roscoe 'Fatty' Arbuckle's career was destroyed, the Hays Office drew up
a list of over two hundred people in the entertainment business who were
considered 'morally dangerous'.

Take 38

1   Which female martial artist starred in *China O'Brien* (1988)?

2   *Children of the Corn* (1984) is adapted from a short story by whom?

3   Name the three male leads in Joel Schumacher's *8mm* (1999)?

4   Oliver Stone wrote the screenplay intending to direct it, but the production ran into financial difficulties. Can you name this 1986 film starring Jeff Bridges, Rosanna Arquette and Andy Garcia?

5   Goldie Hawn and Peter Sellers teamed up in what 1970 comedy?

6   Wesley Snipes and Robert De Niro starred in what Tony Scott film from 1996?

7   Released in 1986, can you name the only other feature from director Robin Hardy of *The Wicker Man* (1973) fame?

8   Richard Harris and Doris Day starred in what comedy thriller from 1967?

9   Name the two male leads in the World War I drama *Gallipoli* (1981)?

10 What was the name of documentarist Nick Broomfield's 1997 film about Kurt Cobain and Courtney Love?

11 Who directed the religious biographical drama *Kundun* (1997), about the Dalai Lama reincarnation?

12 Who starred in *LA Story* (1991)?

13 William Holden starred in what thriller from 1962?

14 Who played the wheelchair-bound architect in the 1998 remake of *Rear Window*?

15 Name the two male leads in Martin Scorsese's film *Mean Streets* (1973).

Answers

1   Cynthia Rothrock

2   Stephen King

3   Nicolas Cage, Joaquin Phoenix and James Gandolfini

4   *8 Million Ways to Die*. Oliver Stone disowned the script and it was doctored by David Lee Henry and Robert Towne

5   *There's a Girl in My Soup*

6   *The Fan*

7   *The Fantasist*, set in Ireland

8   *Caprice*

9   Mark Lee and Mel Gibson. The movie was directed by Peter Weir

10 *Kurt and Courtney*

11 Martin Scorsese

12 Steve Martin. He also wrote the screenplay

13 *The Counterfeit Traitor*

14 Christopher Reeve

15 Robert De Niro and Harvey Keitel

'Cocaine is God's way of saying, you're making too much money.'
– *Robin Williams*

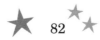

Take 39

1   What was the name of Ali G's 2002 movie?

2   Name the male and female leads in *The Pelican Brief* (1993).

3   *Final Cut* (1998) was directed by Ray Burdis and Dominic Anciano. Name the three leads.

4   Name any of the four leads in *The Piano* (1993)?

5   Who played the sniper/caller in Joel Schumacher's *Phone Booth* (2002)?

6   Who directed *Return of the Jedi* (1983)?

7   Eddie Murphy, Randy Quaid, Rosario Dawson, Joe Pantoliano and Luis Guzman starred in what $100m sci-fi flop from 2001?

8   Katharine Hepburn died on 29 June 2003. How old was she?

9   Name the Robert Altman satirical comedy from 1994 about the fashion industry.

10   Which rocker played the street people leader in John Carpenter's *Prince of Darkness* (1987)?

11   She starred in the erotic sci-fi thriller *Naked Souls* (1995)? What is her name?

12   What was the name of the hit play in Mel Brookes' film *The Producers* (1968)?

13   Who directed the fantasy film *The Never Ending Story* (1984)?

14   Who starred as Gabriel in *The Prophecy* trilogy?

15   Which Californian senator is the star attraction of the documentary *Pumping Iron* (1976)?

Two of Henry Fonda's wives committed suicide.

Answers

1. *Ali G Indahouse*

2. Julia Roberts and Denzel Washington. The movie was adapted from a book by John Grisham

3. Ray Winstone, Jude Law and Sadie Frost

4. Holly Hunter, Harvey Keitel, Sam Neill and Anna Paquin

5. Kiefer Sutherland. The movie also starred Colin Farrell and Forest Whitaker

6. Richard Marquand. The movie was based on a story by George Lucas

7. *Pluto Nash*

8. 96

9. *Prêt a Porter*

10. Alice Cooper

11. Pamela Anderson

12. *Springtime for Hitler*

13. Wolfgang Petersen. It was his first English-speaking movie. But he went on to direct *Shattered* (1991), *In the Line of Fire* (1993) and *Troy* (2004).

14. Christopher Walken in *The Prophecy* (1994), *The Prophecy 2* (1997) and *The Prophecy 3: The Ascent* (2000)

15. Arnold Schwarzenegger

'I was Snow White , but I drifted'
– Mae West

Take 40

1   Who played the misguided politician in *Rabbit-Proof Fence* (2002), Philip Noyce's film set in Australia?

2   Released in 2003, name George Clooney's directorial debut movie.

3   James Caan starred in what sci-fi thriller from 1988?

4   Name the 1949 comedy starring William Bendix?

5   Cary Grant and Grace Kelly starred in what 1955 Hitchcock movie?

6   Yves Montand starred in *Let's Make Love* (1960). Who was his female co-star?

7   Who wrote the screenplay for Michael Cimino's film *Year of the Dragon* (1985), starring Mickey Rourke?

8   Who played quiz kid Donnie Smith in *Magnolia* (1999)?

9   Jason Scott Lee stars in this 1994 film drama about the Moai, the huge stone faces of Easter Island. Name it.

10   Name the classic 1960 western, directed by Antony Mann, starring Glenn Ford and Maria Schell.

11   Who played Malcolm X in Spike Lee's 1992 movie of the same name?

12   Name the two leads in the wrestling comedy *Ready to Rumble* (2000).

13   From whose novel is the film *LA Confidential* (1997) adapted?

14   Who played Dr. Jekyll and Mr. Hyde in *Mary Reilly* (1995)?

15   Al Pacino and Colin Farrell starred in this 2002 spy thriller. Name it.

'If there were a way to make movies without actors, George Lucas would do it.'
— *Mark Hamill*

Answers

1   Kenneth Branagh

2   *Confessions of a Dangerous Mind*, based on TV host Chuck Barris' memoirs of the same title

3   *Alien Nation*

4   *The Life of Riley*

5   *To Catch a Thief*

6   *Marilyn Monroe*

7   Oliver Stone

8   William H. Macy. The movie also starred Julianne Moore, Tom Cruise and John C. Reilly, and was directed by P.T. Anderson

9   *Rapa Nui*, directed by Kevin Reynolds

10   *Cimarron*

11   Denzel Washington

12   David Arquette and Oliver Platt

13   James Ellroy

14   John Malkovich. The movie also starred Julia Roberts, and was directed by Stephen Frears

15   *The Recruit*

'I'm not unduly obsessed with stardom or the industry. The secret to success
is not to fill your mind with your own self-importance.'
– Clint Eastwood

Take 41

1 Which *X-Files* actor starred in *Return to Me* (2000)?

2 Kylie Minogue appeared in what 2001 movie starring Nicole Kidman and Ewan McGregor?

3 Fred Zinneman directed, and Robert Mitchum and Deborah Kerr starred. Name this 1960 movie.

4 Which French actor co-starred in Roland Emmerich's disaster movie *Godzilla* (1997)?

5 Who played Thora Birch's best friend in *American Beauty* (1999), with whom Kevin Spacey becomes obsessed?

6 Sylvester Stallone and Dolly Parton starred in what 1984 comedy about country and western singing?

7 Jack Lemmon and Lee Remick starred in what harrowing 1962 drama directed by Blake Edwards?

8 Which Irish make-up artist won an Oscar for her work on *Cyrano de Bergerac* (1990)?

9 Denzel Washington, John Lithgow and Ice T starred in what action crime movie of 1991 about a deranged killer and the cop tracking him?

10 Name the two male leads in *Bridget Jones Diary* (2001), starring Renée Zellweger.

11 Drew Barrymore starred in what biographical comedy drama from 2001 based on the memoirs of Beverly Donofrio?

12 Who directed the 1998 remake of Alfred Hitchcock's 1960 classic *Psycho*?

13 Which *Baywatch* 'hunk' starred in *Ring of the Musketeers* (1994)?

14 Tom Cruise, Rebecca De Mornay and Joe Pantoliano starred in what comedy from 1983?

15 Nicolas Cage won an Oscar for what 1995 movie?

Answers

1   David Duchovny. The movie also starred Minnie Driver

2   *Moulin Rouge*

3   *The Sundowners*

4   Jean Reno

5   Mena Suvari

6   *Rhinestone*

7   *Days of Wine and Roses*

8   Michèle Burke

9   *Ricochet*

10 Hugh Grant and Colin Firth

11 *Riding in Cars with Boys*

12 Gus Van Sant

13 David Hasselhoff

14 *Risky Business*

15 *Leaving Las Vegas*

'Someone from Warners saw *Death in Venice* and was bowled over by the music.
We told him it was Mahler. "Terrific," he said, "We must sign him."'
– Dirk Bogarde

Take 42

1   Laurence Harvey and Kim Novak starred in what 1964 drama, based on a Somerset Maugham story?

2   *Go* (1999) was a follow up to Doug Liman's first movie. Can you name it?

3   Name the two leads who starred in *The Saint* (1997)?

4   *The Indian Runner* (1991), starring Viggo Mortensen and David Morse, was Sean Penn's directorial debut and was based on which Bruce Springsteen song?

5   Name Oliver Stone's excellent biographical war drama from 1986, starring James Woods and James Belushi.

6   Glenda Jackson played Lady Hamilton and Peter Finch played Lord Horatio Nelson in what 1972 historical drama?

7   The film *Best* (1999) was based on which sporting great?

8   Finish the title of this musical drama from 2000: *Save the* ____ ____.

9   In what year was *Gattaca* starring Ethan Hawke, Uma Thurman and Jude Law made: 1995, 1997 or 1999?

10   Anthony Hopkins, Jane Fonda and Claire Bloom starred in what 1973 movie, based on an Ibsen play?

11   Name the 1973 movie in which a young Tatum O'Neal marked her debut by appearing with her real-life father, Ryan O'Neal?

12   Who played a cameo role as a priest in a send up of *The Exorcist* in *Scary Movie 2* (2001)?

13   Sophia Loren and Marcello Mastroianni starred in what Vittorio de Sica movie from 1964?

14   Who made his directorial debut with *Reality Bites* (1994)?

15   This 2001 crime thriller, directed by Frank Oz, starred Robert De Niro, Edward Norton and Marlon Brando. Name it.

Answers

1. *Of Human Bondage*

2. *Swingers*

3. Val Kilmer and Elisabeth Shue. The movie was directed by Philip Noyce

4. 'Highway Patrolman'

5. *Salvador*

6. *Bequest to the Nation*

7. George Best, the legendary Northern Irish soccer player who set alight English football when playing for Manchester United

8. *Save the Last Dance*. The movie starred Julia Styles and Sean Patrick Thomas

9. 1997

10. *A Doll's House*

11. *Paper Moon*

12. James Woods

13. *Marriage – Italian Style*

14. Ben Stiller. He also directed *Cable Guy* (1996) and *Zoolander* (2001)

15. *The Score*

'Just give me my span of years and knock me down when it's all over.'
– *Lee Marvin*

Take 43

1   In the film credits of US movies what do the initials A.S.C. mean?

2   Rod Steiger starred as a homosexual US army sergeant in this 1968 film. Name it.

3   Alfred Hitchcock directed *The Birds* (1963), but who wrote the original novel?

4   Name the two male stars of *Seven Years in Tibet* (1997)?

5   Name Eric Bogosian's big hit one-man show from Broadway, directed by John McNaughton and released as a movie in 1991.

6   Which 1993 film, starring Danny Glover, Alfred Woodward and Malcolm McDowell, was actor Morgan Freeman's debut as a director?

7   Name the 2000 crime drama which starred Ray Winstone and Ben Kingsley.

8   Who played 'The Shadow' in the 1994 movie of the same title?

9   Who starred opposite Goldie Hawn in the action comedy thriller *Bird on a Wire* (1990)?

10 Name this Richard Attenborough movie from 1993, starring Anthony Hopkins and Debra Winger.

11 Name the two leads in *Jacknife* (1988)?

12 Who played the Oscar-winning lead role in the movie *Shine* (1996)?

13 Name the 1981 French masterpiece about two mixed-up tapes, which marked the directorial debut of Jean-Jacques Beineix.

14 In what modern comedy western did Jack Palance win an Oscar in 1992?

15 Who was the director behind such films as *Airplane* (1980), *Naked Gun* (1988) and *Scary Movie 3* (2003)?

Answers

1   American Society of Cinematographers

2   *The Sergeant*, directed by John Flynn

3   Daphne Du Maurier

4   Brad Pitt and David Thewlis

5   *Sex, Drugs, Rock and Roll*. The movie was filmed at Boston's Wilbur Theatre

6   *Bopha!*

7   *Sexy Beast*, directed by Jonathan Glazer

8   Alec Baldwin

9   Mel Gibson. The movie also starred David Carradine

10   *Shadowlands*

11   Robert De Niro and Ed Harris

12   Geoffrey Rush

13   *Diva*

14   *City Slickers* (1992). This was the longest (40 years) any actor has had to wait between being nominated and actually winning

15   David Zucker

'In my own mind, I'm not sure that acting is something
for a grown man to be doing.'
– *Steve McQueen*

Take 44

1 Who played the part of the philosophical cab driver in Mike Leigh's *All or Nothing* (2002)?

2 Name the writer/director of *Once Upon a Time in Mexico* (2003).

3 Charlize Theron, Mark Wahlberg and Edward Norton starred in the 2003 remake of what 1969 movie?

4 Ed Burns, Rachel Weisz and Dustin Hoffman starred in a stylish thriller directed by James Foley. Name the movie from 2003.

5 Meg Ryan, Jennifer Jason Leigh and Mark Ruffalo starred in what 2003 thriller?

6 Complete the title of this thriller starring Denzel Washington: *Out of ____* (2003).

7 Complete the title of this Ray Bradbury adaptation: *Something Wicked ____ ____ ____* (1983).

8 Who was the male lead in *Soldier* (1998)?

9 Name the 1993 period romantic drama starring Jodie Foster, Richard Gere, Bill Pullman and James Earl Jones.

10 Can you name the 1995 sci-fi horror movie starring Ben Kingsley, Michael Madsen and Natasha Henstridge?

11 Michael Douglas and Andy Garcia appear in what 1989 thriller by Ridley Scott?

12 Chevy Chase and Dan Aykroyd starred in what 1985 comedy directed by John Landis?

13 Can you name the female and male leads in *Labyrinth* (1986)?

14 Who played Stanley and Iris in the 1989 movie of the same name?

15 Name John Carpenter's 1984 sci-fi romance film, starring Jeff Bridges and Karen Allen.

Louis Malle's movie poster for *Les Amants* (1959) was banned
by London Transport as it was deemed to be too obscene.
It showed Rodin's statue of a couple in a tender embrace.

Answers

1   Timothy Spall

2   Robert Rodriguez

3   *The Italian Job*

4   *Confidence*

5   *In the Cut.* The movie was directed by Jane Campion

6   *Out of Time*

7   *Something Wicked This Way Comes*

8   Kurt Russell

9   *Sommersby*

10   *Species.* The movie was directed by Roger Donaldson, and also starred Forest Whitaker

11   *Black Rain*

12   *Spies Like Us*

13   Jennifer Connelly and David Bowie

14   Robert De Niro and Jane Fonda

15   *Starman*

'Life should be a ball.'
– *Victor Mature*

Take 45

1   Wim Wender directed Peter Falk in what movie from 1987?

2   What was James Cagney's character's name in *White Heat* (1949)?

3   What film studio in Rome was famous for producing sword and sandal epics in the late 1950s and early 1960s?

4   What did Woody Allen do before he became an actor, writer and director?

5   The wife (Joan Fontaine) was terrified of being murdered by her husband (Cary Grant) in what psychological thriller from 1941?

6   In what year was *Toy Story* released in the USA?

7   What comic actor played the lead in *Dead Men Don't Wear Plaid* (1982)?

8   Bob Hope and Lucille Ball starred in what movie from 1963?

9   Who played the child prostitute in Martin Scorsese's 1976 movie *Taxi Driver*?

10 Who directed *The Piano* (1993)?

11 Barbra Streisand directed and starred in what 1983 movie?

12 Who worked in a video store before becoming a famous writer, director and actor?

13 Richard Burton and Elizabeth Taylor starred in what 1967 movie, based on a Christopher Marlowe play?

14 She played a memorable cameo in *All About Eve* (1950). Name her.

15 Name John Malkovich's directorial debut movie of 2002.

The longest commercial US movie to date is *Cleopatra* (1963) at 4 hours and 3 minutes. On its release it flopped, almost destroying 20th Century Fox because it had cost a whopping $43 million.

Answers

1 *Wings of Desire*

2 Cody Jarrett

3 Cinecitta Studio

4 He was a stand-up comic and TV gag writer

5 *Suspicion*, directed by Alfred Hitchcock

6 1995

7 Steve Martin

8 *Critic's Choice*

9 Jodie Foster

10 Jane Campion

11 *Yentl*

12 Quentin Tarantino

13 Dr. Faustus

14 Marilyn Monroe

15 *The Dancer Upstairs*

'I'm glad I was born poor; poverty gives me one priceless gift of real ambition.'
– Sophia Loren

Take 46

1   Who was the female lead in *Kill Bill* (2003)?

2   Cameron Diaz and Jim Carrey starred together in what 1994 movie?

3   What was Marlene Dietrich's last movie appearance?

4   What blockbuster movie made over $1 billion at the box office in the USA in 1998?

5   Who directed *Picnic at Hanging Rock* (1975)?

6   What silent movie director was dubbed 'Shakespeare of the screen'?

7   What was Oliver Hardy's nickname?

8   On what 1944 movie set did Humphrey Bogart meet his future wife Lauren Bacall?

9   Name the actress who has a grapefruit pushed into her face by James Cagney in *Public Enemy* (1931).

10   Name the director of *Nosferatu, The Vampire* (1979).

11   He was once Italy's most popular male star, appearing in several romantic comedies opposite Sophia Loren and seen in *La Dolce Vita* (1960). Who was he?

12   Name the famous documentary made by Robert Flaherty in 1922.

13   Who played Henry VIII in *The Private Life of Henry VIII* (1933)?

14   He was a popular performer in the 1930s and 1940s, with prominent teeth, who sang and played the ukelele. Who was he?

15   In what year was *Forrest Gump*, starring Tom Hanks, released: 1990, 1992 or 1994?

'Psychiatry has helped me tremendously as an actress.'
– Joan Collins

Answers

1   Uma Thurman

2   *The Mask*

3   *Just A Gigolo* (1978), opposite David Bowie

4   *Titanic*

5   Peter Weir

6   David Wark Griffith

7   Babe

8   *To Have and Have Not*

9   Mae Clark

10 Werner Herzog

11 Marcello Mastroianni

12 *Nanook of the North*

13 Charles Laughton

14 George Formby

15 1994

'If you want something done right, you have to do it yourself,
as O.J. Simpson says.'
– *Denis Leary*

Take 47

1   Who played the astronaut Dave in *2001: A Space Odyssey* (1968)?

2   Who played football idol Jess in the 2001 comedy *Bend It Like Beckham*?

3   Who played Amélie in the 2001 hit movie of the same name?

4   Who starred in the World War II drama *Play Dirty* (1969)?

5   In *Dirty Harry* (1971) starring Clint Eastwood, what city did detective Dirty Harry Callaghan patrol?

6   What did Alec Nicol do to James Stewart in *The Man From Laramie* (1955)?

7   What was the name of Jack Nicholson's character in *The Shining* (1980)?

8   Who played J.J. Hunsecker in *Sweet Smell of Success* (1957)?

9   What was the first name of Sylvester Stallone's character Rambo in *First Blood* (1982)?

10   Who played Jonathan Harker in Francis Ford Coppola's screen version of Bram Stoker's *Dracula* (1992)?

11   Well known for his role in a TV series based in Hawaii, which actor played a CIA agent in *Dr. No* (1962)?

12   Robert Shaw and Christopher Plummer starred in what historical drama from 1969, based on a Peter Shaffer play?

13   Who won an Oscar for playing Bela Lugosi in *Ed Wood* (1994)?

14   This 1990 western won an Oscar for Best Picture and was the leading actor's directorial debut. Name the film and director.

15   Who played Buddy Holly in the movie *The Buddy Holly Story* (1978)?

'If I had the dough I'd buy up the negative of every film I ever made
and start one hell of a fire.'
– *Sterling Hayden*

Answers

1   Keir Dullea

2   Parminder Nagra

3   Audrey Tautou

4   Michael Caine

5   San Francisco

6   He shot Stewart in the hand while his buddies held him down

7   Jack Torrance

8   Burt Lancaster

9   John

10 Keanu Reeves

11 Jack Lord

12 *The Royal Hunt of the Sun*

13 Martin Landau

14 *Dances With Wolves*, directed by Kevin Costner

15 Gary Busey

'I hate being a teetotaler. I imagine getting up in the morning and knowing
that's as good as you're going to feel all day.'
– Dean Martin

Take 48

1   Who said: 'I'm not bad, I'm just drawn that way.'

2   Who played Bullseye in *Dare Devil* (2003)?

3   Michael J. Fox and Sean Penn starred in what war movie from 1989?

4   Who played Magneto in *The X-Men* (2000)?

5   Who played Jack Nicholson and Shelley Duvall's son in *The Shining* (1980)?

6   Who wrote the novel *The Shining*?

7   Where was *The Bridge on the River Kwai* (1957) set?

8   What was the theme song in the above movie?

9   James Woods played a government agent and Nick Nolte played the local priest in a 2003 movie set in Montana in 1955. Can you name the movie?

10   Who co-starred as Mel Gibson's on-screen brother in *Signs* (2002)?

11   This post-Taliban movie of 2003 was set in Kabul in 2002 and directed by Siddiq Barmak. Can you name it?

12   Who played the serial killer Aileen Wvornos in *Monster* (2003)?

13   Who played the leader of the outlaws in *The Wild Bunch* (1969)?

14   Name the rival teenage gangs in *West Side Story* (1961) .

15   What 1969 movie, directed by Sidney Pollack and starring Jane Fonda and Gig Young, depicted the horrors of the Depression?

Orsen Welles and Peter Sellers detested each other so much
that when they acted together in *Casino Royale* (1967)
they both used doubles when playing opposite each other.

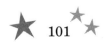

# Answers

1 Jessica Rabbit (Kathleen Turner) in *Who Framed Roger Rabbit?* (1988)

2 Colin Farrell

3 *Casualties of War*

4 Ian McKellen

5 Danny Lloyd

6 Stephen King

7 In Japanese-occupied Burma

8 'The Colonel Bogey March', an old WWI whistling tune

9 *Northfolk – USA*

10 Joaquin Phoenix

11 *Osama*

12 Charlize Theron

13 William Holden

14 The Jets and the Sharks

15 *They Shoot Horses Don't They?*

The most married male star in Hollywood so far was Mickey Rooney,
who was married 8 times.

CINEMA GREATS

Clint Eastwood

1 Released in 1971, what was the first movie Clint Eastwood both directed and acted in?

2 What was Clint's first movie appearance?

3 Name his first western movie from 1958.

4 Clint directed a movie about the legendary jazz musician Charlie Parker. Name the movie and the year it was released.

5 Where was Clint Eastwood born?

6 Complete the title of this Clint Eastwood movie from 1990: *White Hunter, _____ _____*

7 Who starred alongside Clint, pretending to be a nun, in *Two Mules For Sister Sara* (1970)?

8 Who directed *Dirty Harry* (1971)?

9 What is the name of Clint's production company?

10 Complete the title of this Clint Eastwood western from 1972: *Joe _____*

11 Clint Eastwood directed William Holden in a romantic comedy of 1973. Can you name it?

12 In *The Outlaw Josey Wales* (1976) who played Josey's Native American companion?

13 Released in 1973, what was Dirty Harry's second outing in a movie?

14 In *Thunderbolt and Lightfoot* (1974) who was Clint's road buddy?

15 Who played the sadistic prison warden in *Escape From Alcatraz* (1979)?

'If we get the point where I look like a basset hound, I'll just play basset hounds.'
– Clint Eastwood

Answers

1. *Play Misty For Me*

2. *Revenge of the Creature* (1955)

3. *Ambush at Cimarron Pass*

4. *Bird* (1988)

5. San Francisco, USA on May 31 1930

6. *White Hunter, Black Heart*

7. Shirley MacLaine

8. Don Siegel

9. Malpaso

10. *Joe Kidd*

11. *Breezy*

12. Chief Dan George

13. *Magnum Force*

14. Beau Bridges

15. Patrick McGoohan

Clint Eastwood rose to stardom, not along the Hollywood route
but in low-budget westerns shot in Italy. People at the time thought
he was committing professional suicide.

CINEMA GREATS

Clint Eastwood

1 In *High Plains Drifter* (1973) what colour did Clint's character make the townfolk paint the town?

2 In *Paint Your Wagon* (1969) who played the role of wife to Clint and Lee Marvin?

3 In what 1985 movie did Clint play a mysterious preacher who arrives to help gold prospectors?

4 In *Honky Tonk Man* (1982) which popular country and western singer, who made a brief appearance in the movie, died before its release?

5 What was Clint's unusual co-star in *Every Which Way But Loose* (1978) and *Any Which Way You Can* (1980)?

6 Clint played a New Jersey shoe salesman who took over a rundown wild west show in what 1980 movie?

7 Complete this Clint Eastwood movie title from 1970: _____ *Heroes*.

8 Clint played an art teacher called back into service by his former employers, the CIA, and found himself up a dangerous mountain. Name the movie from 1975.

9 In what 1984 movie did Clint star alongside Burt Reynolds?

10 What special award did Clint Eastwood receive in 1985 from the French government?

11 In what year did *Unforgiven* win the Academy Award for best picture?

12 Who played the rookie alongside Clint Eastwood in the movie *Tough Guy* (1990)?

13 What musical instrument is Clint playing in the movie *In the Line of Fire* (1993)?

14 Before Clint became a movie star he was a star in a popular TV western series from the late 1950s to the mid-1960s. Name it.

15 In *The Bridges of Madison County* (1995) who starred opposite Clint as a lonely housewife?

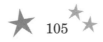

Answers

1   Red

2   Jean Seberg

3   *Pale Rider,* also directed by Clint Eastwood

4   Marty Robbins

5   An orang-utan

6   *Bronco Billy*

7   *Kelly's Heroes*

8   *The Eiger Sanction*

9   *City Heat*

10 He was decorated Chevalier des Arts et Lettres

11 1992

12 Charlie Sheen

13 Jazz piano

14 *Rawhide*

15 Meryl Streep

'The budget for *Apocalypse Now* (1976) was over $25 million, for that sort of money,
we could have invaded somewhere.'
– Clint Eastwood

CINEMA GREATS

Meryl Streep

1   What film gained Meryl Streep her first nomination for an Oscar in 1978?

2   She won a Best Supporting Actress for what divorce drama in 1979?

3   In what 1982 movie did she play a Polish woman who must decide which of her children lived or died?

4   In what year was Meryl Streep born?

5   Complete the title of this Meryl Streep movie: _____-*Devil* (1989).

6   Who were her two co-stars in *Death Becomes Her* (1992)?

7   In what 1977 movie did she make her screen debut?

8   In *Out of Africa* (1985), which writer and farmer did Meryl play?

9   Starring Meryl Streep and Jeremy Irons, on whose novel is *The French Lieutenant's Woman* (1981) based?

10   Who was Meryl Streep's male star in *Ironweed* (1987)?

11   Loosely based on Carrie Fisher's bestseller, what was the 1990 movie starring Meryl and Shirley MacLaine?

12   In what 1983 movie did Meryl play a nuclear plant worker?

13   Name the 1985 movie based on David Hare's play starring Meryl Streep, Charles Dance and Sam Neill.

14   In *A Cry in the Dark* (1988), which real-life character did Meryl play?

15   Based on Isabel Allende's classic novel of the same name, in which 1993 movie did Meryl appear?

"Douglas would be the first man to tell you he's a difficult man.
I would be the second.'
– *Burt Lancaster (on Kirk Douglas)*

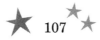

Answers

1   *The Deer Hunter*

2   *Kramer Vs Kramer*

3   *Sophie's Choice*

4   1951, in Basking Bridge, New Jersey, USA

5   *She-Devil*

6   Bruce Willis and Goldie Hawn

7   *Julia*

8   Karen Blixen

9   John Fowles

10 Jack Nicholson

11 *Postcards from the Edge*

12 *Silkwood*

13 *Plenty*

14 Linda Chamberlain, who claimed her baby was killed by a dingo in Australia

15 *The House of the Spirits*

'Acting is just one big bag of tricks.'
– Laurence Olivier

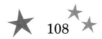

CINEMA GREATS

Meryl Streep

1   Can you name the light romance from 1984 starring Meryl Streep and Robert De Niro?

2   Meryl Streep and Jack Nicholson worked together twice, in 1986 and 1987. What was the comedy they did in 1986?

3   Complete the title of this political thriller from 1979 starring Alan Alda, Barbra Harris and Meryl Streep: *The Seduction of _____ _____.*

4   In what state was *The Bridges of Madison County* (1985) set?

5   In what 2001 science fiction movie, directed by Steven Spielberg, did Meryl Streep appear?

6   Meryl starred in *Dancing at Lughnasa* (1988). Who wrote the acclaimed play this movie was based on?

7   Name the two female leads alongside Meryl in *The Hours* (2002).

8   Spike Jonze directed Meryl Streep and Nicolas Cage in what 2002 satirical comedy?

9   Wes Craven directed Meryl in what movie from 1999? (Surprisingly, it was not a horror movie!)

10 Name the movie from 1996 starring Meryl Streep, Diane Keaton, Leonardo DiCaprio and Robert De Niro.

11 She starred in a thriller in 1982 with Roy Scheider. Name the movie.

12 Liam Neeson starred with her in what 1996 drama about parents whose son was accused of murdering his girlfriend?

13 Meryl plays the mother of an epileptic son in what 1997 movie?

14 In what movie from 1979 did Woody Allen appear with Meryl Streep?

15 Who starred as the main villains giving Meryl a hard time in *The River Wild* (1994)?

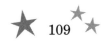

Answers

1   *Falling in Love*

2   *Heartburn*

3   *The Seduction of Joe Tynan*

4   Iowa

5   *AI: Artificial Intelligence*

6   Brian Friel

7   Julianne Moore and Nicole Kidman

8   *Adaptation*

9   *Music of the Heart*

10   *Marvin's Room*

11   *Still of the Night*

12   *Before and After*

13   *First Do No Harm*

14   *Manhatten*, directed by Woody Allen

15   Kevin Bacon and John C. Reilly

'I'm an actor. And I guess I've done so many movies I've achieved some high
visibility. But a star? I guess I still think of myself as kind of a worker ant.'
– Forest Whitaker

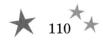

IN THE CAN

Take 1

1   Name Bernardo Bertolucci's most recent movie set in Paris during the 1968 riots.

2   Bill Murray won a 2004 BAFTA award for his role in which movie?

3   Who played American poet Sylvia Plath in *Sylvia* (2004)?

4   Directed by George Lucas, and said to be the last in the series, name this sci-fi adventure to be released in 2005.

5   What 2004 movie was about a football coach, his writer wife and their twelve children?

6   Bugs Bunny and team made a comeback in what 2004 movie, starring Brendan Fraser and Steve Martin?

7   Who wrote and directed *Something's Gotta Give* (2004), starring Jack Nicholson and Diane Keaton?

8   Who gave voice to Garfield in the 2004 movie of the same name?

9   Snoop Dogg starred as Huggy Bear but who played Starsky and Hutch in the 2004 film of the same name as this law-enforcing duo?

10 Who directed *The Passion of the Christ* (2004)?

11 Who was the star of *The Butterfly Effect* (2004)?

12 Name the writer of *Eternal Sunshine of a Spotless Mind* (2004), starring Jim Carrey and Kate Winslet ?

13 *The Day After Tomorrow* (2004) starred Denis Quaid and Jake Gyllenhaal. Can you name the big budget director?

14 Who directed Hugh Jackman in *Van Helsing* (2004)?

15 What actor, who made his name on MTV, starred in *Grand Theft Parsons* (2004)?

'All Englishmen like dresses. It's something in their genes.
Everyone knows it, they just don't talk about it.'
– *David Bowie*

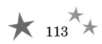

Answers

1   *The Dreamers* (2004)

2   *Lost in Translation*, directed by Sofia Coppola and co-starring Scarlett Johansson

3   Gwyneth Paltrow

4   *Star Wars: Episode III – Revenge of the Sith*

5   *Cheaper By the Dozen*. The movie starred Steve Martin and Helen Hunt

6   *Looney Tunes: Back in Action*

7   Nancy Myers

8   Bill Murray

9   Ben Stiller and Owen Wilson

10   Mel Gibson

11   Ashton Kutcher

12   Charlie Kaufman. He also wrote *Adaptation* (2002) and *Being John Malkovich* (2000)

13   Roland Emmerich

14   Stephen Sommers

15   Johnny Knoxville

'My boyfriend calls me "princess" but I think of myself
more along the lines of "monkey" and "retard".'
– *Alicia Silverstone*

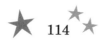

Take 2

1   Who directed *Alexander* (2004), starring Colin Farrell?

2   Orlando Bloom played Liam Neeson's son who fought the invading crusaders in what Ridley Scott movie of 2004?

3   Clive Owen played a Roman warrior in what 2004 movie directed by Jerry Brucheimer?

4   Mel Gibson's Icon Productions have planned their next epic, *The Warrior*, about a ninth century queen. Can you name her?

5   What cult movie from 2002 got a new release in 2004 with plenty of new scenes added?

6   Paul Schrader's planned horror movie is *Exorcist: The Beginning.* Can you give the date release of the original *Exorcist*?

7   Who directed *Paycheck* (2004), starring Ben Affleck?

8   What newcomer starred alongside Nicole Kidman and Anthony Hopkins in *The Human Stain* (2004)?

9   Who directed the *Columbine*-inspired film *Elephant* (2004)?

10   Name the female lead in *Hellboy* (2004).

11   Who played Sirius Black in *Harry Potter and the Prisoner of Azkaban* (2004)?

12   Joaquin Phoenix, William Hurt and Sigourney Weaver starred in what supernatural thriller from 2004?

13   In what western from 2004 did Kevin Costner team up with Robert Duvall?

14   Who replaced the late Richard Harris as Dumbledore in *Harry Potter and the Prisoner of Azkaban* (2004)?

15   What historical figure does Al Pacino plan to play in *The Monster of Longwood* (2004)?

'Oh, yeah, wonderful. Brad and Tom going after the same girl,
ripping her to shreds. Makes you really want to start dating again.'
– *Julia Roberts (on* Interview with the Vampire)

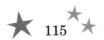

Answers

1. Oliver Stone

2. *Kingdom of Heaven*

3. *King Arthur*

4. Queen Boudicea

5. *Donny Darko* (director's cut)

6. 1973

7. John Woo

8. Wentworth Miller

9. Gus Van Sant

10. Linda Blair, of *Exorcist* fame

11. Gary Oldman

12. *The Village*

13. *Open Range*

14. Michael Gambon

15. Napoleon

'Sting can work on the rainforests. I'll work on the Pepsi cans.'
– Michael J. Fox

Take 3

1   Name Peter Jackson's next project since completing the *Lord of the Rings* trilogy?

2   What western outlaw is Brad Pitt playing in his next movie?

3   Name the actress who played Spider-Man's girlfriend in *Spider-Man 2* (2004)?

4   Name the female star of *Connie and Carla* (2004) who also starred in *My Big Fat Greek Wedding* (2002)?

5   Who starred in *The Cat in the Hat* (2004)?

6   Name the female lead in *Gothika* (2004)?

7   Who starred as a PR man in *People I Know* (2004)?

8   Tom Hanks starred in a remake of a British classic comedy from 1955 that starred Alex Guinness. Name this 2004 comedy.

9   Nicole Kidman and Matthew Broderick star in the 2004 remake of what 1975 movie based on Ira Levin's novel?

10   Who directed *The Company* (2004)?

11   Who played Gabriel Van Helsing in *Van Helsing* (2004)?

12   Bruce Willis teamed up with Matthew Perry in what comedy of 2004?

13   What famous iconic actor died on 1st July 2004?

14   Peter Bogdanovich directed what movie of 2004 about William Randolph Hearst (the inspiration for *Citizen Kane*, 1941)?

15   The Rock plays a modern sheriff in what 2004 movie about corruption in a small town?

'I could rip Madonna's throat out. I can sing better than she can.'
– Meryl Streep

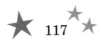

Answers

1. *King Kong*
2. Jesse James
3. Kirsten Dunst
4. Nia Vardalos
5. Mike Myers
6. Halle Berry
7. Al Pacino
8. *The Lady Killers*
9. *The Stepford Wives*
10. Robert Altman
11. Hugh Jackman
12. *The Whole Ten Yards*
13. Marlon Brando
14. *The Cat's Meow*
15. *Walking Tall*

'I adore *Beavis and Butthead*. It is an extraordinary, powerful and important
piece of work. It also makes me laugh like a drain.'
– Patrick Stewart

Take 4

1   William H. Macy and Alec Baldwin starred in what 2004 movie?

2   Who played King Agamemnon in *Troy* (2004)?

3   Name the comic book demon character who has recently hit the big screen?

4   When Viggo Mortensen completed the *Lord of the Rings* trilogy, what was his next movie, released in 2004?

5   Johnny Depp, John Turturro, Maria Bello and Timothy Hutton starred in what 2004 movie based on a Stephen King story?

6   Who voiced Lola in the animation movie *Shark Tale* (2004)?

7   Who voiced Puss in Boots in *Shrek 2* (2004)?

8   Isabelle Adjani and Gerard Depardieu star in what 2004 movie set in Nazi-occupied France?

9   Who directed *King Arthur* (2004)?

10 Which actor died in 2004 after a 64-year career in the movies?

11 Who played the female lead in the comedy *The Girl Next Door* (2004)?

12 She starred as a female boxing promoter in *Against the Ropes* (2004). Name her.

13 What female star appeared in the sci-fi movie *The World of Tomorrow* (2004)?

14 Isabella Rossellini played a musician, who was also a double-amputee, in what 2004 movie?

15 Johnny Depp and John Malkovich starred in what 2004 historical drama?

'In California, they don't throw their garbage away – they make it into TV shows.'
– *Woody Allen*

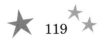

Answers

1 *The Cooler*

2 Brian Cox

3 Hell Boy

4 *Hidalgo*

5 *Secret Window*

6 Angelina Jolie

7 Antonio Banderas

8 *Bon Voyage*

9 Antoine Fuqua. He also directed the Oscar winning *Training Day* (2001)

10 Peter Ustinov (1921–2004)

11 Elisha Cuthbert

12 Meg Ryan

13 Gwyneth Paltrow

14 *The Saddest Music in the World*

15 *The Libertine*

I can't stand the sight of Ronald Reagan. I'd like to stick my Oscar up his ass.'
– Gloria Grahame

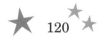

GOLDEN AGE OF HOLLYWOOD

Take 1

1   What American actor used the famous phrase 'I never met a man I didn't like'?

2   Who said the famous line 'I *am* big. It's the pictures that got small!'?

3   Give the first names of the famous comedy team Abbott and Costello.

4   In what 1943 movie did Jayne Russell make her screen debut?

5   What actor was born Joe Yule Junior in Brooklyn, New York City, on 23 September 1920 and went on to be a famous child star and later adult star?

6   Name the 1960 film about a teacher arrested for teaching Darwin's Theory of Evolution, starring Spencer Tracy, Fredric March and Gene Kelly.

7   Who was the voice of Shere Khan in Disney's animated classic *The Jungle Book* (1967)?

8   Who starred as Zola in *The Life of Emile Zola* (1937)?

9   Who played Ophelia to Laurence Olivier's Hamlet in the 1948 movie *Hamlet*?

10 William Holden made his screen debut in what 1938 movie?

11 Who played Mark Twain in the movie *The Adventures of Mark Twain* (1944)?

12 Who directed *The Ten Commandments* (1923)

13 Cary Grant and Tony Curtis starred in what comedy from 1959?

14 Who played the devious Delilah in *Samson and Delilah (1949)*?

15 Who played legendary lawman Wyatt Earp in *Gunfight at the OK Corral* (1957)?

'Bruce Willis, The World's Worst Actor.'
– *Robert Stephens*

Answers

1   Will Rogers
2   Gloria Swanson in *Sunset Boulevard* (1950), directed by Billy Wilder
3   Bud Abbott and Lou Costello
4   Howard Hughes's *The Outlaw*. The film was banned for two years because the critic at the time considered it the ultimate in licentiousness
5   Mickey Rooney
6   *Inherit the Wind*, directed by Stanley Kramer
7   George Sanders
8   Paul Muni
9   Jean Simmons
10   *Golden Boy*
11   Frederic March
12   Cecil B. DeMille, who also directed the 1956 version starring Charlton Heston
13   *Operation Petticoat*
14   Hedy Lamarr. The movie was directed by Cecil B. DeMille
15   Burt Lancaster. The movie also starred Kirk Douglas as the doomed Doc Holliday

Cecil B. DeMille was obsessed with historical accuracy. He sent his art director to Egypt to find out the exact colour of the pyramids before filming *Cleopatra* (1934). The art director returned explaining, just as they predicted, that the pyramids were sandy brown in colour. The movie was filmed in black and white!

Take 2

1   Who played Robin Hood in *The Adventures of Robin Hood* (1938)?

2   What Irish actor played the male lead in Sean O'Casey's screen adaptation of *Juno and the Paycock* (1930)?

3   Who played Lincoln in the film *Young Mr. Lincoln* (1939)?

4   In *The Big Heat* (1953) who starred as the dogged detective?

5   Who played the artist Toulouse-Lautrec in *Moulin Rouge* (1952)?

6   What comic genius once quipped: 'No one who hates dogs and children can be all that bad'?

7   'Top of the world Ma' were the final words screamed by James Cagney as he shoots at a gas container and blows himself up. What was the 1949 movie title?

8   Ava Gardner, Tyrone Power and Errol Flynn starred in what 1957 version of an Ernest Hemingway novel?

9   Who played Sergeant Fatso Judson and beat Frank Sinatra to death in *From Here to Eternity* (1953)?

10   Who played the damsel in distress in the 1933 version of *King Kong*?

11   Who created the cartoon comedy duo Tom and Jerry?

12   Orson Welles famously began his film career in *Citizen Kane* (1941), loosely based on what real life character?

13   Sidney Lumet has directed close to fifty films in his career, but what brilliant 1957 courtroom drama did he direct to make his name?

14   What is so significant about the opening scene in *Touch of Evil* (1958), starring Charlton Heston, Janet Leigh and Orson Welles?

15   Gary Cooper and Audrey Hepburn starred in what 1957 romantic comedy set in Paris and directed by Billy Wilder?

'I have these slumber parties with my father
and when we can't sleep we stay up all night trading beauty tips.
He knows all about the good creams and masks.'
– *Liv Tyler (on Aerosmith's Steve Tyler)*

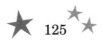

Answers

1 Errol Flynn. The legendary medieval outlaw was originally supposed too be played by James Cagney

2 Barry Fitzgerald

3 Henry Fonda

4 Glenn Ford. Directed by Fritz Lang, the movie also starred Lee Marvin and Gloria Grahame

5 José Ferrer. The movie was directed by John Huston and featured Zsa Zsa Gabor and can-can dancer Jane Avril

6 W.C. Fields

7 *White Heat*, directed by Raoul Walsh

8 *The Sun Also Rises*

9 Ernest Borgnine. Directed by Fred Zinnemann, the movie also starred Burt Lancaster and Deborah Kerr

10 Fay Wray

11 Fred Quimby, William Hanna and Joseph Barbera. (*Tom and Jerry* films over the years won seven Oscars.)

12 Randolph Hearst

13 *Twelve Angry Men,* directed by Sidney Lumet

14 It is a continuous shot lasting three minutes and fifteen seconds – a very long time to act out in one take. Consider this: the average shot on screen only lasts seven seconds

15 *Love in the Afternoon*

'It's a job – someone's gotta do it. The reality is Jennifer and I can do our job well because we truly are friends. But when the day's over, she goes home to her boyfriend and I go home to a magazine.'
– *David Schwimmer (on kissing Jennifer Aniston)*

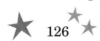

Take 3

1   Judy Holliday won an Oscar in 1950 playing a dumb blonde. What was the film?

2   What was Bob Hope's theme song?

3   Who was known as 'the golden boy' in the early 1940s?

4   Who starred as the male trapeze artist in Cecil B. DeMille's *The Greatest Show on Earth* (1952)?

5   Who began his film career as the grinning psychotic killer in *Kiss of Death* (1947)?

6   A critic once said of her: 'She couldn't act, she couldn't dance, she couldn't sing, but boy could she swim!' Who was he describing?

7   Who was the child star in *The Courage of Lassie* (1946), and went on to become a major Hollywood star?

8   In the 1930s and 1940s they were dubbed the big four movie gangsters. Can you name them?

9   Who starred in *Adventures of Don Juan* (1948)?

10 What famous movie star died while filming a duel scene in *Solomon and Sheba* (1958)?

11 Who played Captain Ahab in the movie *Moby Dick* (1956), directed by John Huston?

12 The most famous group of star children from the 1920s and 1930s was known as?

13 Who played the black-clad killer who confronts Alan Ladd in *Shane* (1953)?

14 Who starred as the leather-clad biker in *The Wild One* (1953)?

15 Who played General Rommel in *The Desert Fox* (1951) and *The Desert Rats* (1953)?

'Wet Esther Williams is a star, dry she ain't.'
– *Joe Pasternak*

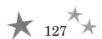

Answers

1. *Born Yesterday*. Holliday was Columbia's fifth choice to play the part, after Rita Hayworth, Jan Sterling, Gloria Grahame and Evelyn Keyes

2. 'Thanks for the Memory' – a song he sang with Shirley Ross in his first feature *The Big Broadcast* (1938)

3. William Holden, who began his career in a film of that title *Golden Boy* (1939).

4. Cornel Wilde. The movie also has surprise appearances by Dorothy Lamour, Bob Hope and Bing Crosby

5. Richard Widmark

6. Esther Williams

7. Elizabeth Taylor

8. James Cagney, Humphrey Bogart, Edward G. Robinson and George Raft

9. Errol Flynn

10. Tyrone Power, who died from a heart attack. The film was completed with Yul Brynner as Power's replacement

11. Gregory Peck

12. *Our Gang*. Their first film was *One Terrible Day* (1922)

13. Jack Palance

14. Marlon Brando. Directed by Laslo Benedek, the movie also featured Lee Marvin

15. James Mason

Buddy Ebsen, best remembered for the TV series *Beverly Hillbillies*, was the original tin man in *The Wizard Of Oz* (1939) but was replaced by Jack Haley after nine days because he had been poisoned by his make-up.

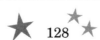

Take 4

1 What was Elvis Presley's first movie?

2 Ingrid Bergman and Charles Boyer starred in what melodrama from 1944, directed by George Chucker?

3 Name the seven actors who starred in *The Magnificent Seven* (1960)?

4 Mario Lanza and Kathryn Grayson starred in what musical from 1949?

5 What comic genius played the actor-manager in the film *To Be or Not to Be* (1942)?

6 Who played the original Cisco Kid in the 1931 movie of the same title?

7 Alan Ladd and his son David appeared together in what 1958 movie?

8 Ray Milland won an Oscar for what movie from 1945?

9 What movie star was dubbed 'The Look' and was married to Humphrey Bogart?

10 Gregory Peck starred with Jane Wyman in what movie from 1946?

11 Who was known as the first Hollywood singing cowboy?

12 Who was considered the greatest dancer in the history of cinema, and starred in such movies as *Top Hat (1938)*, *Silk Stockings (1957)* and *The Band Wagon (1953)*?

13 What two-time Olympic champion swimmer went on to star as Tarzan in *Tarzan the Ape Man* (1932)?

14 Humphrey Bogart and Fredric March starred in what thriller from 1955?

15 In the movie *Harvey* (1950), what was James Stewart's invisible friend?

'I should never have married, but I didn't want to live without a man.
Brought up to respect the conventions, love had to end in marriage.
I'm afraid it did.'
– *Bette Davis*

Answers

1. *Love me Tender* (1956)
2. *Gaslight*
3. Yul Brynner, Steve McQueen, Robert Vaughn, Horst Buchholz, James Coburn, Charles Bronson and Brad Dexter
4. *That Midnight Kiss*
5. Jack Benny. The movie was directed by Ernst Lubitsch
6. Warner Baxter
7. *The Proud Rebel*
8. *The Lost Weekend*, directed by Billy Wilder
9. Lauren Bacall
10. *The Yearling*
11. Gene Autry
12. Fred Astaire
13. Johnny Weissmuller, cinema's sixth Tarzan, scooped a total of five gold medals at the 1924 and 1927 Olympics
14. *The Desperate Hours*
15. A giant white rabbit

'Killing an animal to make a coat is a sin. It wasn't meant to be and we have no right to do it. A woman gains status when she refuses to see anything killed to be put on her back. Then she's truly beautiful!'
– *Doris Day*

Take 5

1   Name the 1962 western that was a fitting conclusion to the two careers of top western stars Joel McCrea and Randolph Scott.

2   How many times did Boris Karloff play Frankenstein's monster?

3   What comic actor played the lead role in *The Secret Life of Walter Mitty* (1947)?

4   Who starred in *Singing in the Rain* (1952), the title song becoming his theme tune?

5   Who played the governess in *The Innocents* (1962)?

6   Who played the female lead in *Dial M for Murder* (1954), directed by Alfred Hitchcock?

7   Who played the female lead in *This Gun for Hire* (1942)?

8   Who directed *The Treasure of the Sierra Madre* (1948)?

9   Who became one of the hottest properties in Hollywood after her performance as a deaf mute in *Johnny Belinda* (1948)?

10 Who was known as 'The Sweater Girl' of World War Two?

11 Who was dubbed 'The Beautiful Hunk of a Man' in the 1940s?

12 Can you name the leading actor in *A Time to Love and A Time to Die* (1958), based on a novel by E.M. Remarque, who also wrote *All Quiet on the Western Front*?

13 Who played Harry Lime in Carol Reed's *The Third Man* (1949)?

14 Billy Wilder directed what classic romantic comedy from 1954 starring Humphrey Bogart, William Holden and Audrey Hepburn?

15 Who were the young lovers in *A Place in the Sun* (1951)?

'He taught me housekeeping; when I divorce I keep the house.'
– *Zsa Zsa Gabor (on her ex-husband)*

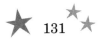

Answers

1   *Ride the High Country,* directed by Sam Peckinpah. It was also known as *Guns in the Afternoon*

2   Three times: *Frankenstein* (1931), *Bride of Frankenstein* (1935) and *Son of Frankenstein* (1939)

3   Danny Kaye

4   Gene Kelly

5   Deborah Kerr

6   Grace Kelly

7   Veronica Lake

8   John Huston. The movie starred Humphrey Bogart and Walter Huston

9   Jane Wyman

10   Lana Turner

11   Victor Mature

12   John Gavin

13   Orson Welles. The movie was directed by Carol Reed

14   *Sabrina*

15   Elizabeth Taylor and Montgomery Clift

'The problem with people who have no vices is that generally you can be pretty sure they're going to have some pretty annoying virtues.'
– *Elizabeth Taylor*

Take 6

1   Born Norma Jean Mortensen, she went onto become one of the great sex symbols and stars of Hollywood. Who was she?

2   What British actress played the female lead in *A Streetcar Named Desire* (1951), from the play by Tennesse Williams?

3   Who starred as the intrepid traveller Phileas Fogg in Mike Todd's *Around the World in 80 Days* (1956)?

4   Who played Sir Launcelot in *Knights of the Round Table* (1953)?

5   In what 1940 Laurel and Hardy movie did Peter Cushing have a cameo role?

6   Directed by Nicholas Ray, *Rebel Without a Cause* (1955), starring James Dean, launched which female lead to stardom?

7   *Baby Doll* (1956), based on a story by Tennesse Williams and directed by Elia Kazan, starred which female as the child-wife?

8   Who played Natasha in Tolstoy's *War and Peace* (1956) directed by King Vidor?

9   In *Lust for Life* (1956), Kirk Douglas played Vincent Van Gogh. Who played Gauguin?

10 In Ingmar Bergman's *The Seventh Seal* (1957), who played the knight?

11 Who played Porgy and Bess in the 1959 film of the same name?

12 He played the Roman officer rescued by Charlton Heston in *Ben-Hur* (1959). Can you name him?

13 Stewart Granger and Peter Ustinov starred in what movie from 1954, about a regency dandy?

14 John Wayne played the Ringo Kid in a 1939 movie and finally became a star after ten years of B-movies. Name the movie.

15 Who played the female lead in *The Song of Bernadette* (1943)?

Answers

1. Marilyn Monroe
2. Vivien Leigh
3. David Niven
4. Robert Taylor
5. *Chumps at Oxford*
6. Natalie Wood
7. Carroll Baker
8. Audrey Hepburn
9. Anthony Quinn
10. Max Von Sydow. The movie was shot in only 35 days
11. Sidney Poitier and Dorothy Dandridge
12. Jack Hawkins
13. *Beau Brummell*
14. *Stagecoach*, directed by John Ford
15. Jennifer Jones. The movie also starred Charles Bickford and Vincent Price

'If you obey all the rules, you miss all the fun.'
– Katharine Hepburn

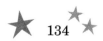

Take 7

1 In what year was the classic *King Kong* made: 1929, 1931 or 1933?

2 Who played the title role in the western *Shane* (1953)?

3 Who played the crooked insurance man in Billy Wilder's *Double Indemnity* (1944)?

4 Esther Williams' last big movie was with Cliff Robertson and Robert Vaughn in 1961. Can you name it?

5 He played the condemned prisoner who started a prison riot in *The Last Mile* (1959). Name him.

6 Who starred in *The Nun's Story* (1958)?

7 Who played the devil-worshipping medieval prince in Roger Corman's movie *The Masque of the Red Death* (1964)?

8 Who did Orson Welles marry and appear alongside in the movie *The Lady from Shanghai* (1948)?

9 What child actor was the No. 1 box office attraction from 1935 to 1938?

10 Who played the Roman legionnaire in *Quo Vadis* (1951) opposite Deborah Kerr, the Christain slave he fell in love with?

11 Who played career girl Laura in the 1944 movie of the same title?

12 What was Spencer Tracy's last movie?

13 Maria Schell played Grushenka in *The Brothers Karamazov* (1958), but who publicly declared that she wanted the role?

14 Bette Davis, Paul Henreid and Claude Rains starred in what melodrama from 1946?

15 Rex Harrison played a muslim leader and George Sanders played Richard the Lionheart in what historical epic from 1954?

'You name it and I've done it. I'd like to say I did it my way.
But that line, I'm afraid, belongs to someone else.'
– *Sammy Davis Junior*

Answers

1   1933
2   Alan Ladd
3   Fred Mac Murray. The female lead was played by Barbara Stanwyck
4   *The Big Show*
5   Mickey Rooney
6   Audrey Hepburn
7   Vincent Price
8   Rita Hayworth
9   Shirley Temple
10 Robert Taylor
11 Gene Tierney. The movie also starred Dana Andrews, Clifton webb, Vincent Price and Judith Anderson
12 *Guess Who's Coming to Dinner?* (1967)
13 Marilyn Monroe
14 *Deception*
15 *King Richard and the Crusaders*, from the Walter Scott novel *The Talisman*

In *Wuthering Heights* (1939) the Yorkshire moors was filmed just outside Hollywood, with heather brought in for the close-ups.

Take 8

1   In 1965 Julie Andrews won her first Academy Award for what classic Disney family movie?

2   Who starred as Jean Lafitte in the 1938 swashbuckler *The Buccaneer*?

3   Humphrey Bogart, Bette Davis and Leslie Howard starred in what thriller from 1936?

4   Carroll Baker, George Peppard and Alan Ladd starred in what movie from 1964?

5   Charles Laughton directed only one movie; it starred Robert Mitchum as a villainous preacher. What was the 1954 movie?

6   Harry Belafonte and Joan Fontaine starred in what 1957 drama?

7   Humphrey Bogart won an Academy Award in what 1951 movie?

8   Name the 1955 medical drama starring Robert Mitchum, Olivia de Havilland, Frank Sinatra and Gloria Grahame.

9   Boris Karloff, Wallace Ford and Victor McLaglen starred in a World War I drama from 1934. Can you name it?

10   What was the name of the 1951 biopic of Britain's pioneer of the cinema, William Friese-Greene, starring Robert Donat?

11   Joan Crawford teamed up with Clark Gable as a mistress to a politician. Name this 1931 movie.

12   Who played Pollyanna in the 1960 movie of the same name?

13   Charlton Heston played Buffalo Bill Cody in what western of 1953?

14   Name Fritz Lang's harrowing movie from 1946 about Nazism.

15   Who starred in *The Razor's Edge* (1946), based on W. Somerset Maugham's story?

'Attempt the impossible in order to improve your work.'
– Bette Davis

Answers

1   *Mary Poppins*, in which she played the practically perfect Edwardian nanny
2   Frederic March
3   *The Petrified Forest*
4   *The Carpet Baggers*. This was Alan Ladd's last movie
5   *The Night of the Hunter*
6   *Island in the Sun*
7   *The African Queen*, directed by John Huston. The movie also starred Katharine Hepburn
8   *Not As a Stranger*
9   *The Lost Patrol*
10   *The Magic Box*
11   *Possessed*
12   Hayley Mills
13   *Pony Express*
14   *Hangmen Also Die*
15   Tyrone Power. It also starred Gene Tierney, John Payne and Anne Baxter

'Everybody's a mad scientist, and life is their lab. We're all trying to experiment to find a way to live, to solve problems, to fend off madness and chaos.'
– David Cronenberg

CINEMA GREATS

Marlon Brando

1. Released in 1950, what was Marlon Brando's first movie?

2. Brando played Stanley Kowalski in what 1951 movie based on a Tennessee Williams play of the same name?

3. Which character did Brando play in *Julius Caesar* (1953)?

4. Brando was first nominated for an Academy Award for what movie?

5. In what comedy from 1998 did Brando played Sven the Swede ?

6. Brando produced, directed and starred in what 1961 movie?

7. Which historical figure did Brando portray in *Désirée* (1950)?

8. Name Brando's two American co-stars in *The Young Lions* (1958).

9. Charlie Chaplin directed Brando and Sophia Loren in what 1967 movie?

10. Brando won Oscars in which two movies?

11. In which 1978 movie did Brando play a superhero's father?

12. Who directed Brando in *Last Tango in Paris* (1972)?

13. Brando was nominated as best Supporting Actor in which 1989 movie?

14. In what year did Brando star in *Apocalypse Now*: 1970, 1978 or 1979?

15. Brando played a cowboy alongside Jack Nicholson in what 1976 movie?

'Acting is the expression of a neurotic impulse. It's a bum's life.
Quitting acting, that's a sign of maturity.'
– *Marlon Brando*

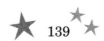

Answers

1	*The Men*
2	*A Streetcar Named Desire*
3	Marc Antony
4	*A Streetcar Named Desire* (1951)
5	*Free Money*
6	*One-Eyed Jacks*
7	Napoleon
8	Montomery Clift and Dean Martin
9	*A Countess From Hong Kong*
10	*On the Waterfront* (1959), and *The Godfather* (1972)
11	*Superman*
12	Bernardo Bertolucci
13	*A Dry White Season*
14	1979
15	*The Missouri Breaks*

'Like most Catholic boys, I wanted to be Jesus Christ. I could never
get the turn-the-other-cheek thing down, though.'
– Jim Carrey

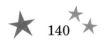

CINEMA GREATS

Marlon Brando

1   In what 1955 musical did Brando star with Jean Simmons and Frank Sinatra?

2   Complete the title of a Brando movie from 1963: *The _____ American*.

3   In *Reflection in a Golden Eye* (1967), which female co-starred with him?

4   Brando played a modern sheriff in what 1966 movie set in South America?

5   Brando starred in a crime thriller in 1968 wearing a blond wig. The movie co-starred Richard Boone and Rita Moreno. Can you name it?

6   What part did Brando play in *Mutiny on the Bounty* (1962)?

7   Brando acted in a comedy in 1964 with David Niven. Can you name it?

8   Tyrone Power was supposed to play the lead, but it went to Brando. Name the 1952 movie about a revolutionary leader.

9   Brando returned to the westerns to star in a 1966 movie about a stolen horse. Name the movie.

10   Brando played a Japanese interpreter in what 1956 movie which co-starred Glenn Ford?

11   Johnny Depp starred with Brando in what 1995 movie?

12   Can you name the 1990 comedy, co-starring Matthew Broderick, in which Brando played a self-parody of the Godfather?

13   Name the 1980 thriller co-starring George C. Scott about a Nazi process for creating synthetic fuel, in which Brando plays a tycoon.

14   Name the 2001 crime drama starring Brando, Robert De Niro and Edward Norton.

15   Brando worked again with Trevor Howard after their clashes on *Mutiny on the Bounty* in a 1965 spy drama. Name the movie.

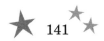

Answers

1. *Guys and Dolls*

2. *The Ugly American*

3. Elizabeth Taylor

4. *The Chase*

5. *The Night of the Following Day*

6. Fletcher Christian

7. *Bedtime Story*

8. *Viva Zabata!*, co-starring Anthony Quinn

9. *The Appaloosa*, also known as *Southwest to Sonora*

10. *The Teahouse of the August Moon*

11. *Don Juan De Marco*

12. *The Freshman*

13. *The Formula*

14. *The Score*

15. *The Saboteur, Code Name Morituri*, co-starring Yul Brynner

'The only gossip I'm interested in is things from the *Weekly World News* –
Woman's bra bursts, 11 injured – that kind of thing.'
– *Johnny Depp*

SILENT ERA

Take 1

1 Who played the first screen Tarzan in *Tarzan of the Apes* (1918)?

2 What was the first American storyline movie in 1903?

3 In the 1914 serial *The Perils of Pauline* who played Pauline?

4 Regarded as one of his best, name this 1924 Buster Keaton comedy.

5 Who played Aramand in *Camille* (1920)?

6 Who directed *Broken Blossoms* (1919)?

7 He played the Thief of Bagdad in the 1924 movie of the same name? Who was he?

8 Who starred as the British Prime Minister Disraeli in the 1929 movie of the same title?

9 Who was the male lead in *Flesh and the Devil* (1926)?

10 He played Don Juan in the 1926 movie of the same title. Name him.

11 Who starred as Scaramouche in the 1923 movie of the same title?

12 Which son of a famous actor made his screen debut in *Stephen Steps Out* (1923)?

13 Name the 1923 western about the opening of the West.

14 What was the name of the famous cross-eyed comic actor from the silent screen?

15 Who became a star after he appeared in *The Prisoner of Zenda* (1922)?

Europe's largest cinema, known as the Gaumont Palace, was opened in Paris in 1931. It could seat 5,000 people in its auditorium.

Answers

1 Elmo Lincoln

2 *The Great Train Robbery*

3 Pearl White. The first movie in the series was released in 1914

4 Sherlock Junior

5 Rudolph Valentino. His leading lady was Alla Nazimova

6 D.W. Griffith. The movie starred the exceptional Lillian Gish

7 Douglas Fairbanks Senior

8 George Arliss, at the age of 61

9 John Gilbert

10 John Barrymore

11 Ramon Navarro

12 Douglas Fairbanks Junior. Only fifteen at the time, he went on to have a successful career of his own

13 *The Covered Wagon*

14 Ben Turpin

15 Ramon Navarro

'Happiness is good health and a bad memory.'
– Ingrid Bergman

Take 2

1 Released in 1921, what was Rudolph Valentino's first major film role?

2 Which actress and swimmer appeared nude in *Daughters of the Gods* (1916)

3 What was Rin Tin Tin?

4 Which actress was dubbed the most popular star in silent movies?

5 Silent matinee idol Ivor Novello was born in what British city: Cardiff, London or Glasgow?

6 Who starred in the silent version of *Ben-Hur* (1926)?

7 Who was known as 'King of the Cowboys' in the 1920s?

8 Who was the king of suspense comedy in the silent movies?

9 Who played the evil doctor in *The Cabinet of Doctor Caligari* (1919)?

10 Who rivalled Charlie Chaplin as the greatest silent film comedian?

11 Three actors got together in 1919 to form United Artists Corporation. Who were they?

12 Who was billed as the greatest boy actor in the world in the silent films?

13 Who was the top animated star in the 1920s?

14 Who was known as 'King of the Swashbucklers'?

15 Who was the first great horror film star?

The story goes that the practice of stars leaving their prints outside the famous Grauman's Theatre began on May 18 1927 when a famous actress accidentally stepped on wet cement outside the theatre. This gave Sid Grauman the idea to start this celebrity hall of fame, thinking it might be a good publicity stunt. It certainly was!

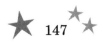

Answers

1   *The Four Horsemen of the Apocalypse*, directed by Rex Ingram

2   Annette Kellerman

3   A German Shepherd dog, who became the biggest animal star in the 1920s. Rin Tin Tin starred in more than 40 films and received an average of 12,000 fan letters per week

4   Mary Pickford

5   He was born Ivor Novello Davies in Cardiff, South Wales in 1893

6   Ramon Novarro

7   Tom Mix

8   Harold Lloyd

9   Werner Krauss

10   Buster Keaton

11   Mary Pickford, Douglas Fairbanks Senior and Charlie Chaplin (along with director D.W. Griffith and manager Hiram Abrams)

12   Jackie Coogan, co-starring with Charlie Chaplin in *The Kid* (1921) at the age of five. He stayed at the top for ten years

13   Felix the Cat

14   Douglas Fairbanks Senior

15   Lon Chaney Senior

'I'm disappointed in acting as a craft. I want everything to go back to Orson Welles and fake noses and changing your voice. It's become so much about personality.'
– Skeet Ulrich

Take 3

1   Who was billed as the world's greatest actor in the 1920s and the greatest screen lover?

2   Who was known as the first movie star and appeared in *The Great Train Robbery* (1903)?

3   Who was dubbed 'The Vamp' and played the lead in *Cleopatra* (1917)?

4   Which silent comic star's career was destroyed after a scandal in which he was accused of the manslaughter of a young girl at a Labour Day party?

5   Who was known as the first movie star actress?

6   Which actress once described herself as 'every inch and every moment a star'?

7   Who played the female lead in *Pandora's Box* (1929)?

8   Who played the sinister robot in Fritz Lang's *Metropolis* (1926)?

9   The Keystone Cops were the brainchild of what comedy king director?

10   Regarded as the greatest single performance in the history of silent films, who played the title role in *The Passion of Joan of Arc* (1928)?

11   Who played the hideously smiling victim in Paul Lenis' *The Man Who Laughs* (1928)?

12   Complete the name of this famous director of the silent era: Erich Von _____

13   Which actor portrayed the first Frankenstein monster on screen?

14   In what year was the first film version of *Quo Vadis* seen?

15   What was Greta Garbo's country of origin?

'Every actor in his heart believes everything bad that's printed about him.'
– *Orson Welles*

Answers

1   John Barrymore

2   Gilbert M. 'Broncho Billy' Anderson

3   Theda Bara, born Theodosia Goodman

4   Roscoe 'Fatty' Arbuckle, who although acquitted by a jury was never forgiven by the cinema-going public

5   Florence Lawrence

6   Gloria Swanson

7   Louise Brooks

8   Brigitte Helm

9   Mack Sennett

10 Renée Marie Falconetti. The movie was directed by Carl Dreyer

11 Conrad Veidt

12 Erich Von Stroheim

13 Charles Ogle in *Frankenstein or The Modern Prometheus* (1910)

14 This Italian version was first shown in New York's Broadway to an enthusiastic audience in 1913

15 Sweden

For his tramp costume, Charlie Chaplin borrowed Fatty Arbuckle's baggy pants and boots belonging to Ford Sterling. The boots were size 14 and Chaplin had to wear them on the opposite feet to keep them on, thus creating the funny walk. He borrowed the derby and the waistcoat too. The only item belonging to Chaplin was the whangee cane.

Take 4

1   Who played Beau in *Beau Geste* (1926)?

2   Who directed *The Iron Horse* (1924)?

3   Which female actor starred in *The Scarlet Letter* (1926)?

4   In what year did Valentino die?

5   In what 1928 'silent' movie could Al Jolson be heard singing for the first time?

6   Who played the villainous Messala in the 1926 version of *Ben-Hur*?

7   What actor became a cowboy film star after his first film *The Bargain* (1914)?

8   One of Hollywood's most enduring stars became a star following her lead role as Elsie Stoneman in D.W. Griffith's *Birth of a Nation* (1915). Who was she?

9   What leading movie star's career was allegedly destroyed with the coming of sound?

10 Name the sex goddess of American cinema who became Paramount's biggest star in 1927 and 1928?

11 What 1926 production was released as the first commercial two-toned technicolour movie, starring Douglas Fairbanks Senior?

12 In what 1928 movie did Charlie Chaplin appear inside a cage with real lions?

13 Gloria Swanson starred in what 1928 movie, based on W. Somerset Maugham's steamy novel *Rain*?

14 In what year was the formal opening of the famous Sid Grauman's Chinese Theatre in Hollywood?

15 What was the first movie premiered in the above theatre?

'Failure is inevitable. Success is elusive.'
– Steven Spielberg

Answers

1. Ronald Colman
2. John Ford. Charles Edward Bull played the part of Lincoln.
3. Lillian Gish
4. 1926
5. *The Jazz Singer*
6. Francis X. Bushman
7. William S. Hart
8. Lillian Gish
9. John Gilbert, whose acting style was considered too intense to bear the weight of words. He died in 1936 at the age of 40
10. Clara Bow, the beauty who had 'It'
11. *The Black Pirate*
12. *The Circus*
13. *Sadie Thomson*. Lionel Barrymore co-starred
14. May 19 1927
15. Cecil B. DeMille's *King of Kings* (1927)

The first black actor to play a leading role
was Sam Lucas in *Uncle Tom's Cabin* (1914).

HORROR

Take 1

1 Jean Marais and Josette Day starred in *La Belle et la Béte* (1946). Who was the director?

2 Who directed *Frankenstein* (1931)?

3 Who played Dr. Phibes in *The Abominable Dr. Phibes* (1971)?

4 *Merry Frolics of Satan* (1906) featured many strange monsters including an articulated apocalyptic horse. Name the director who pioneered the horror genre.

5 Whose skull did Peter Cushing wish to possess in the film *The Skull* (1965)?

6 There have been several versions of the story *The Island of Dr. Moreau*, but who wrote the original tale?

7 In 1885 Robert Louis Stevenson wrote the famous story *Dr. Jekyll and Mr. Hyde*. Who starred in the Paramount film of 1931?

8 Roman Polanski directed and starred in a comedy-horror in 1967. Can you name it?

9 Who played the vampire Camilla in Hammer's *The Vampire Lovers* (1970)?

10 What well-known star played in MGM's screen version of *Dr. Jekyll and Mr. Hyde* (1941)?

11 What 1957 Hammer film teamed Peter Cushing and Christopher Lee for the first time?

12 What famous comedy duo met Dr. Jekyll and Mr. Hyde in a 1953 Universal movie?

13 What Jewish legend was made into a movie in 1920, which was directed by and starred Paul Wegener?

14 Who directed the classic silent film *Nosferatu* (1922)?

15 'I am Dracula, I bid you welcome.' Who said these immortal words in Tod Browning's *Dracula* (1931)?

Answers

1   Jean Cocteau

2   James Whale

3   Vincent Price

4   Georges Méliès

5   The skull of the Marquis de Sade

6   H.G. Wells

7   Fredric March

8   *Dance of the Vampire,* also known as *The Fearless Vampire Killers*

9   Ingrid Pitt

10   Spencer Tracy

11   *The Curse of Frankenstein*

12   *Abbott and Costello Meet Dr. Jekyll and Mr. Hyde*

13   *The Golem*

14   F.W. Murnau

15   Bela Lugosi

Dracula is the most frequently played monster from literature on the silver screen.

Take 2

1 Who played *The Wolfman* in the 1941 Universal movie of the same name?

2 Who played the son in *Son of Frankenstein* (1938)?

3 Who played Ygor in the above movie?

4 Describe 'Them' in the movie *Them* (1953).

5 What was Tod Browning's last horror movie, made in 1936?

6 A most attractive vampire fiend appeared in Hammer's *Dracula Prince of Darkness* (1965). Who was she?

7 Who played Countess Dracula in Hammer's 1970 film of that title?

8 Bela Lugosi flayed Boris Karloff alive in what 1934 movie?

9 In 1932 Boris Karloff created another classic screen monster. What was the movie?

10 This 1940 movie was Victor Mature's second and launched him as a star. It also introduced Lon Chaney Junior to a wider movie audience. Name the movie.

11 Who played Oscar Wilde's Dorian Grey in MGM's *The Picture of Dorian Grey* (1945)?

12 Who played Dracula in *House of Dracula* (1945)?

13 Bela Lugosi returned as Dracula in what 1943 movie?

14 Peter Cushing, playing Van Helsing, and Christopher Lee, playing Count Dracula, met for the last time on screen in 1972. Name the Hammer movie.

15 Ernest Borgnine was attacked by very unwelcome visitors in the movie *Willard* (1970). What were they?

'For those who understand no explanation is needed.
For those who don't none will do.'
– *Jerry Lewis*

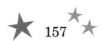

Answers

1   Lon Chaney Junior

2   Basil Rathbone

3   Bela Lugosi

4   Giant ants, the unexpected result of atomic bomb testing

5   *The Devil Doll*. Tod Browning died in 1962, a man forgotten by the film industry

6   Barbara Shelley

7   Ingrid Pitt

8   *The Black Cat,* also known as *House of Doom*

9   *The Mummy*

10 *One Million BC,* also known as *Man and His Mate* and *Cave Dwellers*

11 Hurd Hatfield, with George Sanders, Donna Reed and Angela Landsbury

12 John Carradine

13 *The Return of the Vampire*

14 *Dracula AD 1972*

15 Hordes of rats

'I've just got to maintain my passion for what I do.'
– *Leonardo DiCaprio*

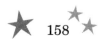

Take 3

1   It was 19th century Cornwall and a young woman turned into a snake after being cursed by some Malaysian sect. What was the 1966 film?

2   Vincent Price, Peter Lorre, Boris Karloff and a young Jack Nicholson starred in a 1963 film based on Edgar Allan Poe's poem. Name the movie.

3   In *The Tingler* (1959), directed by William Castle, what was the Tingler?

4   Name the male and female leads in *The Omen* (1976).

5   What was Mighty Joe Young in the 1949 movie of the same title?

6   Charles Laughton, Boris Karloff, Raymond Massey, Lilian Bond and Melvyn Douglas starred in *The Old Dark House* (1932). Who directed it?

7   In *The Exorcist II: The Heretic* (1977), who played the priest?

8   Who directed *The Fog* (1980)?

9   Who starred in *I Was a Teenage Werewolf* (1957) and went on to be a successful TV star in *Bonanza* and *Little House on the Prairie*?

10   Who was Dr. Moreau in the 1977 version of the movie *The Island of Dr. Moreau*?

11   Basil Rathbone played Richard III, Boris Karloff played Mord and Vincent Price played the Duke of Clarence. Name this 1939 movie.

12   A Shakespearean actor (Vincent Price) fakes his own death then proceeds to murder those that criticised him and gave him bad reviews. What was the 1973 movie?

13   What 1990 film, directed by Tom Savini, was a remake of a 1968 horror classic?

14   Who plays the American novelist in *To the Devil a Daughter* (1976), based on a novel by Dennis Wheatley?

15   Who directed *13 Ghosts* (1960)?

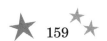

Answers

1. *The Reptile*, directed by John Gilling
2. *The Raven*, directed by Roger Corman
3. A parasitic monster created by fear, which snaps the spinal column of victims unless the person screams
4. Gregory Peck and Lee Remick. Damien was played by Harvey Stevens
5. A twelve-foot gorilla
6. James Whale
7. Richard Burton. The movie was directed by John Boorman
8. John Carpenter
9. Michael Landon
10. Burt Lancaster
11. *The Tower of London*
12. *Theatre of Blood*
13. *Night of the Living Dead*
14. Richard Widmark
15. William Castle

'Run for office? No. I've slept with too many women, I've done too many drugs, and I've been to too many parties.'
– *George Clooney*

Take 4

1   Who was *The Witchfinder General* (1968)?

2   In what year was Stanley Kubrick's *The Shining* made?

3   Who played Count Dracula in the comedy-horror *Vampira* (1974)?

4   Who starred in *Murders in the Rue Morgue* (1971), based on a story by Edgar Allan Poe?

5   Complete the title of the 1969 movie *The _____ Box,* starring Vincent Price and Christopher Lee.

6   Name the German actor who starred in such horror films as *The Man Who Could Cheat Death* (1959), *Circus of Horrors* (1960) and *The Beast Must Die* (1974)?

7   Name the director of such films as *Shivers* (1974), *Rabid* (1976), *The Brood* (1979) and *Scanners* (1980).

8   Name the male and female leads in *The Mephisto Waltz* (1971)?

9   Who starred in *London After Midnight* (1927)?

10 Professor Van Helsing (Peter Cushing) went to China in 1904 only to discover Dracula's disciples were terrorising a village. What was the 1974 movie?

11 *The Devil Rides Out* (1968) starred Christopher Lee as Dennis Wheatley's hero Duc de Richeliev. Who starred as his powerful antagonist?

12 Who played the werewolf in *The Curse of the Werewolf* (1961)?

13 Who starred in *The Curse of the Crimson Altar* (1968)?

14 Name the American actor in *Night of the Demon* (1956)?

15 Robert Quarry brought a new vampire to the screen in 1970. What was the movie called?

'Being a celebrity is probably the closest to being a beautiful woman
as you can get.'
– *Kevin Costner*

Answers

1   Vincent Price

2   1980. The movie starred Jack Nicholson – 'Here's Johnny'

3   David Niven

4   Jason Roberts

5   *The Oblong Box*

6   Anton Diffring

7   David Cronenberg

8   Alan Alda and Jaqueline Bisset

9   Lon Chaney Senior

10   *The Legend of Seven Golden Vampires*

11   Charles Gray

12   Oliver Reed

13   Boris Karloff and Christopher Lee

14   Dana Andrews

15   *Count Yorga, Vampire*

'I have to remind my dad, "Journalists – no matter how many cigars they smoke
with you – are not your friends, so don't talk to them.'"
– Cameron Diaz

Take 5

1. According to Eric Red, the screenwriter of *The Hitcher* (1986), the movie was based on which famous Doors song?

2. Which popular popstar of the 1980s makes an appearance in *Blade II* (2002)?

3. Who wrote and co-starred in Robert Rodriguez cult movie *From Dusk 'til Dawn* (1995)?

4. Who directed Arnold Schwarzenegger in the sci-fi horror *Predator* (1986)?

5. Complete the title of Wes Craven's previously banned movie *The Last House ____ ____ ____* (1972).

6. Can you name the two low-budget films director Peter Jackson made in 1989 and 1992?

7. Which TV series is *Reign of Fire* (2001) director Rob Bowman most noted for directing?

8. Who directed the chilling *Henry: Portrait of a Serial Killer* (1986)?

9. Name the director of *Manhunter* (1986), based on the novel *Red Dragon*. Was it Michael Mann or Brett Ratner?

10. Who wrote the screenplay for the supernatural horror *Dreamcatcher* (2003), starring Morgan Freeman?

11. Name the 2002 horror movie starring Stuart Townsend and singer Aaliyah.

12. In the movie *Village of the Damned* (1995), what happened to make the village damned?

13. Jennifer Lopez, Ice Cube, Eric Stoltz and Jon Voight starred in what 1997 horror adventure?

14. Who directed Bill Pullman in *The Serpent and the Rainbow* (1987)?

15. Who played the lead in the 1986 remake of *The Fly*?

'Because young men are so goddamn disappointing!'
– *Harrison Ford (on why women like older leading men)*

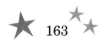

Answers

1. 'Riders on the Storm.' The film starred Rutger Hauer, making one man's journey an absolute nightmare
2. Luke Goss, one half of pin-up boy band Bros
3. Quentin Tarantino
4. John McTiernan
5. *The Last House on the Left*
6. *Bad Taste* and *Brain Dead*
7. *X-Files*
8. John McNaughton
9. Michael Mann. Brett Ratner directed the (2002) remake, with Anthony Hopkins reprising his role as Hannibal Lector
10. William Goldman, who has written many Oscar-winning films and some great books about the movie business
11. *Queen of the Damned*. Aaliyah was killed in a plane crash shortly after the film was completed
12. There was a total blackout and the women awoke pregnant with children of alien origin
13. *Anaconda*
14. Wes Craven
15. Jeff Goldblum

'He's probably the world's most beautiful looking man, yet he doesn't think he's that gorgeous. And to me, he's just smelly, farty Leo.'
– *Kate Winslet (on Leonardo DiCaprio)*

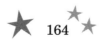

Take 6

1   Who played the phantom in *The Phantom of the Opera* (1925)?

2   Who played Professor Van Helsing in *Dracula* (1931)?

3   'Find something no one else can do and they'll begin to take notice of you.' Who gave these words of advice to Boris Karloff when he was starting out on his career?

4   Who played Nosferatu in the Werner Herzog's 1979 remake of the 1922 silent classic?

5   Who played Abraham Van Helsing in John Badham's *Dracula* (1979)?

6   Complete the title of the Peter Cushing/Christopher Lee movie
    Dr. _____ _____ _____ _____ (1964).

7   Name the 1973 horror movie set mainly in Venice and starring Donald Sutherland and Julie Christie.

8   Following the success of *The Horror of Dracula* (1958), Peter Cushing turned up for a second chance to play Van Helsing in 1960. Name that movie.

9   Who starred in *The Man With the X-Ray Eyes* (1963), directed by Roger Corman?

10 Who directed the comedy-horror *Young Frankenstein* (1974)?

11 Who played the female lead in *The Witches* (1966)?

12 In 1943 Lon Chaney Junior played Count Alucard in what movie?

13 What was Lon Chaney Senior dubbed?

14 Eric Porter starred in what 1971 Hammer movie set in late nineteenth century London?

15 Richard E. Grant was the witchfinder hunting Julian Sands in what 1989 horror film?

'Good judgement comes from experience.
Sometimes, experience comes from bad judgement.'
– Christian Slater

Answers

1   Lon Chaney Senior. The movie was adapted from the novel by Gaston Leroux

2   Edward Van Sloan

3   Lon Chaney Senior

4   Klaus Kinski, with Isabella Adjani co-starring

5   Laurence Olivier

6   The complete title is *Dr. Terror's House of Horror*

7   *Don't Look Now*, adapted from a short story by Daphne Du Maurier

8   *The Brides of Dracula*, directed by Terence Fisher

9   Ray Milland

10   Mel Brooks

11   Joan Fontaine

12   *Son of Dracula*. Alucard is Dracula spelt backwards!

13   The Man with a Thousand Faces

14   *Hands of the Ripper*

15   *Warlock*

'Success is like death. The more successful you become, the higher the houses
in the hills get and the higher the fences get.'
– *Kevin Spacey*

Take 7

1 Who played the policeman in *The Wickerman* (1973)?

2 Name the two famous female Hollywood stars paired in *Whatever Happened to Baby Jane* (1962)?

3 Complete the 1969 film title starring Vincent Price, Christopher Lee and Peter Cushing: *Scream_____ _____ _____*

4 Who directed *Rosemary's Baby* (1968)?

5 The 1971 prequel to *The Innocents* (1961) starred Marlon Brando and Stephanie Beacham. Name the movie.

6 Which *Lord of the Rings* star played a cameo role as the Devil in *The Prophecy* (1994), starring Christopher Walken?

7 What 1986 horror comedy starred singer Grace Jones?

8 Who played the male and female leads in Paul Verhoeven's *Hollowman* (2000)?

9 Vincent Price starred in what 1963 movie based on Nathaniel Hawthorne's short stories?

10 Who starred in *The Hands of Orlac* (1960)?

11 Peter Cushing and Ray Milland starred together in what horror movie from 1977?

12 Can you name the voodoo drama from 1971 starring Shirley MacLaine?

13 Tony Curtis appeared in what horror movie from 1977 about the reincarnation of a 400-year-old Indian witch doctor?

14 Who starred in *The Man Who Cannot Cheat Death* (1959)?

15 Name the 1964 movie, starring Peter Cushing, Christopher Lee and Barbara Shelley, in which villagers were turned into stone.

'I called him Ernie, for he was no rock!'
– *Doris Day (on Rock Hudson)*

Answers

1	Edward Woodward
2	Bette Davis and Joan Crawford
3	*Scream and Scream Again*
4	Roman Polanski
5	*The Nightcomers*
6	Viggo Mortensen
7	*Vamp*
8	Kevin Bacon and Elisabeth Shue
9	*Twice Told Tales*
10	Mel Ferrer and Christopher Lee
11	*The Uncanny*
12	*The Possession of Joel Delaney*
13	*The Manitou*
14	Anton Diffring
15	*The Gorgon*

'I really lived life to its fullest and that got me in trouble from time to time.'
– *Matthew Perry*

MUSICALS

Take 1

1   Name the 1960 Elvis Presley movie in which he sang 'Wooden Heart'?

2   Who was the singer who played Sandy Olsson in *Grease* (1978)?

3   Leonard Bernstein, Stephen Sondheim and Jerome Robbins collaborated on an adaptation of Shakespeare's *Romeo and Juliet,* resulting in what 1961 musical?

4   Who played King Arthur in *Camelot* (1967)?

5   Name the Doris Day western/comedy musical from 1953?

6   Cliff Richard starred in what road movie musical from 1962?

7   Name the 1942 musical, set in the 1890s, starring Rita Hayworth, Victor Mature and Phil Silvers, detailing the life of popular songwriter Paul Dresser.

8   What was the 1972 musical drama based on the writer Christopher Isherwood's *Berlin Memoirs* chronicling the rise of Hitler?

9   Name the classic musical from 1952 starring Gene Kelly, Debbie Reynolds and Donald O'Connor.

10 Can you name the 1964 movie that country singer Jim Reeves made before his untimely death in a plane crash?

11 Catherine Zeta Jones won an Oscar for her role in what 2003 musical?

12 In what year was the classic Beatles animated musical *Yellow Submarine* made?

13 Name the 1965 musical, set in the 1930s, about the Von Trapp family.

14 Name the 1968 musical adapted from a Charles Dickens novel and directed by Carol Reed.

15 G.B. Shaw's *Pygmalion* was turned into what popular musical in 1964?

'Retire? I'm going to stay in show business until I'm the only one left.'
– George Burns (at the age of 90)

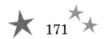

Answers

1   *GI Blues*

2   Olivia Newton-John. Her beau was played by John Travolta

3   *West Side Story*, directed by Robert Wise

4   Richard Harris

5   *Calamity Jane*. The movie also starred Howard Keel

6   *Summer Holiday,* directed by Peter Yates

7   *My Gal Sal*

8   *Cabaret*, starring Liza Minnelli and Michael York

9   *Singing in the Rain*

10   *Kimberley Jim*

11   *Chicago.* The movie also starred Renée Zellweger and Richard Gere

12   1968

13   *The Sound of Music,* starring Julie Andrews and Christopher Plummer

14   *Oliver*, starring Oliver Reed and Ron Moody. The part of Oliver was played by Mark Lester

15   *My Fair Lady*, with Audrey Hepburn and Rex Harrison

The musical *Oklahoma* (1955) was filmed in Arizona!

Take 2

1   Marlon Brando, Jean Simmons and Frank Sinatra starred in what classic musical from 1955?

2   Who directed and starred in *On the Town* (1949)?

3   What dancing duo starred in *Top Hat* (1935)?

4   What 1964 Beatles movie saw Wilfrid Brambell as Grandfather?

5   Name the 1973 musical set in New York with a reworking of St. Matthew's Gospel and a Christ-like figure in a Superman sweatshirt?

6   Who created the story for the animated musical drama *The Nightmare Before Christmas* (1993)?

7   Ian Fleming, author of James Bond, wrote what 1968 musical fantasy starring Dick Van Dyke?

8   Name the 1950 Betty Grable musical starring Victor Mature and Phil Harris.

9   Who played the multiple parts in *Tales of Hoffman* (1951)?

10 Who played the female star with Fred Astaire in *Funny Face* (1956)?

11 *Anna and the King* (1999), starring Jodie Foster, was a remake of what musical of 1956?

12 In what 1996 musical did Madonna play the lead role?

13 Who directed the 1969 musical satire *Oh, What a Lovely War*?

14 Gordon MacRae, Shirley Jones and Rod Steiger starred in what 1955 western musical?

15 Who played the lead in *Fiddler on the Roof* (1971)?

'I wanted revenge; I wanted to dance on the graves of a few people who made me unhappy. It's a pretty infantile way to go through life – I'll show them – but I've done it, and I've got more than I ever dreamed of.'
Anthony Hopkins

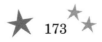

Answers

1   *Guys and Dolls*, directed by Joe Mankiewicz

2   Gene Kelly

3   Fred Astaire and Ginger Rogers

4   *A Hard Day's Night*, directed by Richard Lester

5   *Godspell*

6   Tim Burton. The movie was directed by Henry Selick

7   *Chitty Chitty Bang Bang*, directed by Ken Hughes

8   *Wabash Avenue*

9   Robert Helpmann. The movie was directed by Michael Powell

10   Audrey Hepburn

11   *The King and I*

12   *Evita*, co-starring Antonio Banderas

13   Richard Attenborough. This was his first film as a director

14   *Oklahoma*, directed by Fred Zinnemann

15   Topol

'The key to immortality, is living a life which is worth being remembered.'
– Bruce Lee

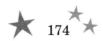

Take 3

1   Who was the 'cover girl' in the 1944 movie of the same title?

2   Complete the Judy Garland movie title *Meet Me in* _____
    _____(1944).

3   Who played Frederic Chopin in *A Song to Remember* (1945)?

4   The Monkees were dandruff in Victor Mature's hair in what zany
    movie of 1968?

5   Who played Don Quixote in *Man From La Mancha* (1972)?

6   Neil Diamond and Laurence Olivier starred in what film from 1980?

7   Richard O'Brien's long running stage play was turned into a movie in
    1975, starring Tim Curry and Susan Sarandon. Can you name it?

8   Who starred in the 1976 remake of *A Star is Born*?

9   What was the name of Martin Scorsese's 1977 movie, starring Liza
    Minnelli and sax-playing Robert De Niro, set in the 1940s?

10 Who starred in the reverential biopic on Elvis in 1979?

11 Name the loosely disguised biopic from 1979 on the late Janis Joplin,
    starring Bette Midler.

12 Who starred in *All that Jazz* (1979) and was nominated for an Oscar?

13 She was a welder by day and an exotic dancer by night. Name the
    1983 movie and its leading star.

14 What was the Andrew Lloyd Webber and Tim Rice groundbreaking
    musical from 1973?

15 What was the all-black (1978) version of *The Wizard of Oz* called,
    starring Diana Ross and Michael Jackson?

'Hollywood is a place where they'll pay you 50,000 dollars for a kiss
and 50 cents for your soul.'
– *Marilyn Monroe*

Answers

1   Rita Hayworth. The movie also starred Gene Kelly

2   *Meet Me in St. Louis*, directed by Vincente Minnelli

3   Cornel Wilde

4   *Head*

5   Peter O'Toole. The movie also starred Sophia Loren and was directed by Arthur Miller

6   *The Jazz Singer*

7   *The Rocky Horror Picture Show*

8   Barbra Streisand and Kris Kristofferson

9   *New York, New York*

10   Kurt Russell

11   *The Rose*, directed by Mark Rydall

12   Roy Scheider. The movie was directed by Bob Fosse

13   *Flashdance*, starring Jennifer Beals

14   *Jesus Christ Superstar*

15   *The Wiz*, directed by Sidney Lumet

'I'm still the little southern girl from the wrong side of the tracks
who really didn't feel like she belonged.'
– Faye Dunaway

Take 4

1 Complete the title of the movie *Annie Get Your* _____ (1950).

2 Her last film for MGM was called *Summer Stock* (1950), starring Gene Kelly and Phil Silvers. Name the star.

3 Who starred in *Lullaby of Broadway* (1951)?

4 Who played the tenor Enrico Caruso in *The Great Caruso* (1951)?

5 In the third screen version of *Showboat* in 1951, who played Ravenal?

6 Who played Danny Wilson in *Meet Danny Wilson* (1952)?

7 Who starred in *Meet Me at the Fair* (1952)?

8 Complete the title of this western musical from 1954: *Seven Brides* _____ _____ _____

9 Name the top money-making film of 1954, starring Bing Crosby, Danny Kaye and Rosemary Clooney.

10 Doris Day teamed with Frank Sinatra for what 1955 movie?

11 Liberace played a self-centered concert pianist who became deaf. Name this 1955 movie.

12 Who played Gigi in the 1958 musical of the same name?

13 Who starred in *Song Without End* (1960)?

14 What 1960 musical starred Dean Martin and Judy Holliday?

15 Frank Sinatra, Shirley MacLaine and Louis Jourdan starred in what 1960 musical?

'If I die before my cat, I want a little of my ashes put in his food
so I can live inside him.'
– *Drew Barrymore*

Answers

1 *Annie Get Your Gun*

2 Judy Garland

3 Doris Day

4 Mario Lanza. The movie was directed by Richard Thorpe

5 Howard Keel. The movie also starred Kathryn Grayson and Ava Gardner

6 Frank Sinatra

7 Dan Dailey

8 *Seven Brides for Seven Brothers*

9 *White Christmas*

10 *Young at Heart*

11 *Sincerely Yours*

12 Leslie Caron. The movie also starred Louis Jourdan and Maurice Chevalier

13 Dirk Bogarde

14 *Bells Are Ringing*, directed by Vincente Minnelli

15 *Can-Can*

'I'd never go to a movie where the leading man has bigger tits
than the leading lady'
– *Groucho Marx (on Victor Mature and Hedy Lamarr in* Samson and Delilah*)*

1 Ken Russell directed the 1975 film version of The Who's *Rock Opera*. Name it.

2 Who starred in *For the First Time* (1959) about an opera singer who falls for a deaf girl?

3 Name the two female leads in the 1967 musical *Millie*?

4 Who starred in *Doctor Dolittle* (1968)?

5 Name the 1963 musical comedy starring Janet Leigh, Ann-Margaret and Dick Van Dyke.

6 Who directed Fred Astaire in *Finian's Rainbow* (1968)?

7 Jason Robards, Britt Ekland, Forrest Tucker and Norman Wisdom starred in what 1968 movie about the birth of striptease?

8 Who played Willie Wonka in *Willie Wonka and the Chocolate Factory* (1971)?

9 Which model made her film debut in *The Boyfriend* (1972)?

10 Sissy Spacek starred as Loretta Lynn while Beverly D'Angelo played Patsy Cline. Can you name this 1980 musical?

11 Released in 1956, what was the first rock 'n' roll movie to star Bill Haley and The Comets?

12 This 1976 movie was the biography of folk singer Woodie Guthrie and starred David Carradine. Can you name it?

13 What pop band starred in *Sergeant Pepper's Lonely Heart's Club Band* (1978)?

14 In what 1965 film did Elvis Presley fall in love with the daughter of a Chicago mobster?

15 Pat Boone, Tommy Sands and Gary Crosby starred in what 1958 musical?

'Jane has survived more bad movies than any actress
should be able to in a lifetime.'
– *Henry Fonda (on his daughter)*

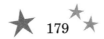

Answers

1   *Tommy*

2   Mario Lanza

3   Julie Andrews and Mary Tyler Moore. The movie was directed by
    George Roy Hill

4   Rex Harrison, Samantha Eggar and Richard Attenborough. The
    movie was directed by Richard Fleischer

5   *Bye Bye Birdie*

6   Francis Ford Coppola

7   *The Night They Raided Minsky's*

8   Gene Wilder

9   Twiggy. The movie, directed by Ken Russell, also starred
    Christopher Gable and Barbara Windsor

10   *Coal Miner's Daughter*. The movie also starred Tommy Lee Jones

11   *Rock Around the Clock*

12   *Bound for Glory*

13   The Bee Gees. The movie also starred Peter Frampton

14   *Girl Happy*

15   *Mardi Gras*

The worst sin you could commit in my family was buying retail.'
– *Woody Allen*

Take 6

1   Name the Bobby Darin jazz musical from 1961.

2   Name the 1961 Rogers and Hammerstein Broadway movie about a Hong Kong bride who arrives in San Francisco for an arranged marriage.

3   What 1942 muscial comedy teamed Victor Mature with Lucille Ball?

4   Elvis starred with Carolyn Jones and Walter Matthau in what musical drama from 1958?

5   Released in 1966, what was Buster Keaton's last movie?

6   Name the 1958 movie in which a middle-aged baseball fan makes a pact with the devil.

7   Name the male and female leads in *South Pacific* (1958)?

8   Who played Tom Thumb in the 1958 musical of the same name?

9   Name the 1959 movie about a legendary cornet player, starring Danny Kaye and Louis Armstrong.

10 What 1959 movie was based on the cartoon character created by Al Capp?

11 Shirley Jones starred with Pat Boone in what 1957 musical?

12 In what year was *Variety Girl,* starring Bob Hope, Bing Crosby and William Holden, released: 1947, 1957 or 1959?

13 Who played the female lead in *Kiss Me Kate* (1953), starring Howard Keel?

14 Name the two dancing stars of *The Band Wagon* (1953)?

15 Name the 1974 compilation of MGM musical moments that was a big hit with cinema goers.

'She ran the whole gamut of emotions from A to B.'
– Dorothy Parker (on Katharine Hepburn's acting)

Answers

1   *Too Late the Blues*, directed by John Cassavetes

2   *Flower Drum Song*

3   *Seven Days' Leave*

4   *King Creole*

5   *A Funny Thing Happened on the Way to the Forum*

6   *Damn Yankees*

7   Rossano Brazzi and Mitzi Gaynor

8   Russ Tamblyn. The movie also starred Peter Sellers and Terry Thomas

9   *The Five Pennies*

10   *Li'l Abner*

11   *April Love*

12   1947

13   Kathryn Grayson

14   Fred Astaire and Cyd Charisse

15   *That's Entertainment*

'I started at the top and worked down.'
– Orson Welles

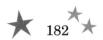

Take 7

1   Featuring Cliff Richard and The Shadows, name this 1961 musical comedy.

2   What was the 1967 musical portrayal of the life of Gertrude Lawrence, starring Julie Andrews?

3   Who played Fanny Brice in *Funny Girl* (1968)?

4   Judy Garland and James Mason starred in what 1954 musical?

5   Who were the two female stars in *Gentlemen Prefer Blondes* (1953)?

6   In what year was *Wizard of Oz*, starring Judy Garland, made: 1939, 1941 or 1945?

7   What was the classic song Judy Garland sang in *Wizard of Oz*?

8   Name the 1943 musical starring Betty Grable, George Montgomery and Cesar Romero.

9   Who starred in *Yankee Doodle Dandy* (1942)?

10 Name the two leads in *For Me and My Gal* (1942)?

11 In what 1945 movie did Gene Kelly dance with Jerry (of *Tom and Jerry* fame)?

12 Who starred as vaudevillian Al in *The Jolson Story* (1946)?

13 Bing Crosby and Fred Astaire were first seen together in *Holiday Inn* (1942). They were re-united in 1946 for what musical?

14 Who played Glenn Miller in *The Glenn Miller Story* (1954)?

15 In what movie of 1948 did Fred Astaire and Judy Garland sing the duet 'A Couple of Swells'?

'An actor's a guy who, if you ain't talking about him, he ain't listening.'
– *Marlon Brando*

Answers

1   *The Young Ones*

2   *Star*

3   Barbra Streisand. The movie was directed by William Wyler

4   *A Star Is Born*

5   Marilyn Monroe and Jane Russell. The movie was directed by Howard Hawks

6   1939

7   'Over the Rainbow'

8   *Coney Island*

9   James Cagney

10 Judy Garland and Gene Kelly

11 *Anchors Aweigh*. The movie also starred Frank Sinatra

12 Larry Parks

13 *Blue Skies*

14 James Stewart. The movie was directed by Antony Mann

15 *Easter Parade*

'Make up your mind, dear boy, do you want to be a great actor or a household word.'
– Laurence Olivier (to Richard Burton)

Take 8

1. In 1962 what long-running Broadway hit musical went on the big screen and starred Rosalind Russell, Natalie Wood and Karl Malden?

2. Elvis played a dual role in what 1964 musical?

3. Name the 1965 musical based on the life of Hank Williams, starring George Hamilton.

4. Name the two leads in *Carousel* (1956)?

5. Bing Crosby, Grace Kelly and Frank Sinatra starred in what charming musical from 1956?

6. Who was the female star in *Sweet Charity* (1969)?

7. Peter O'Toole starred with what female singer in the musical remake of *Goodbye Mr. Chips* (1969)?

8. What was Disney's first live action musical fantasy from 1961?

9. Who played Riff, the leader of the Jets, in *West Side Story* (1961)?

10. What was Al Jolson's follow-up to *The Jazz Singer* (1927) a year later?

11. Released in 1967, what was Walt Disney's last film before he died?

12. What English pop singer starred in *Half a Sixpence* (1967)?

13. Susan Hayward, Rory Calhoun and David Wayne starred in what musical drama from 1952?

14. Can you name the 1951 musical in which Fred Astaire danced on the walls and ceiling of a hotel room?

15. Who starred with Gene Kelly in *An American in Paris* (1951)?

'Actors should be treated like cattle.'
– *Alfred Hitchcock*

Answers

1 *Gypsy*

2 *Kissin' Cousins*

3 *Your Cheatin' Heart*, in which Hank Williams Junior sang the songs for the movie

4 Gordon MacRae and Shirley Jones

5 *High Society*

6 Shirley MacLaine. The movie was directed by Bob Fosse

7 Petula Clark

8 *Babes in Toyland*

9 Russ Tamblyn. The movie was directed by Robert Wise and Jerome Robbins

10 *The Singing Fool*

11 *The Happiest Millionaire*

12 Tommy Steele

13 *With a Song in My Heart*

14 *Royal Wedding* also known as *Wedding Bells*

15 Leslie Caron. The movie was directed by Vincente Minnelli

'Look Richard. I'm the Ham around here so tone it down.'
– *Victor Mature (on offering friendly advice to Richard Burton who was being too theatrical in front of the cameras during the filming of* The Robe)

WESTERNS

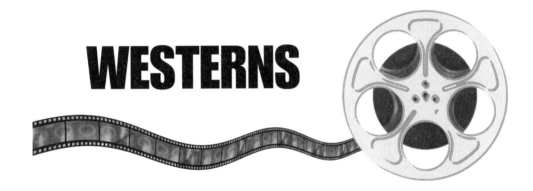

Take 1

1   Name the 1966 western that Jack Nicholson starred in, co-produced and wrote the script for?

2   Who starred in *Day of the Evil Gun* (1968)?

3   Name the famed 'Dollar' trilogy from the 1960s, starring Clint Eastwood.

4   William Holden, Eleanor Parker and Joan Forsythe starred in what western from 1953, directed by John Sturges?

5   Who said: 'A man's gotta do what a man's gotta do'?

6   Name Dean Martin and Jerry Lewis's western comedy of 1956.

7   Who starred in *The Grey Fox* (1982)?

8   Who was Tom Horn in the 1980 movie of the same name?

9   David Carradine starred along with his brothers in what 1980 movie?

10   Audie Murphy played a gunslinger hired to kill a rancher in what 1953 western?

11   Complete the film title: *Buffalo Bill and the Indians or* _____ _____ _____ _____ (1975).

12   Fred MacMurray and James Coburn starred in what western from 1959?

13   Name the western from 1973 starring Burt Reynolds and Sarah Miles.

14   In what contemporary western of 1972 did Lee Marvin and Paul Newman star?

15   Who played the old scout in *Ulzana's Raid* (1972)?

'If someone was dumb enough to offer me a million dollars to make a movie,
I certainly was not dumb enough to turn it down.'
– *Elizabeth Taylor*

Answers

1 *Ride the Whirlwind*

2 Glenn Ford

3 *A Fistful of Dollars* (1964), *For a few Dollars More* (1965) and *The Good, the Bad and the Ugly* (1966)

4 *Escape from Fort Bravo*

5 Alan Ladd says it in *Shane* (1953). The movie was directed by George Stevens

6 *Pardners*

7 Richard Farnsworth

8 Steve McQueen

9 *The Long Riders*. The movie also featured brothers Dennis and Randy Quaid, and Stacy and James Keach. The Carradine brothers were David, Keith and Robert

10 *Gunsmoke*

11 . . . *Sitting Bull's History Lesson*. The movie was directed by Robert Altman

12 *Face of a Fugitive*

13 *The Man Who Loved Cat Dancing*

14 *Pocket Money*

15 Burt Lancaster

The tallest American leading man to date is James Arness at 6'7", famous for his TV show *Gunsmoke*.

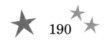

Take 2

1   What one-time Tarzan played Raquel Welch's husband and got shot before the opening credits in *Bandolero* (1968)?

2   What famous rock and roll singer starred in *The Fastest Guitar Alive* (1967)?

3   This 1967 film marked Clint Eastwood's triumphant return to Hollywood after Italy. What was it called?

4   It was deemed a remake of *Rio Bravo* (1959) and starred John Wayne and Robert Mitchum. What was the 1967 film?

5   Jeff Bridges and Sam Waterston starred in what 1975 comedy western?

6   Complete this movie title directed by Raoul Walsh and starring Troy Donahue: *A _____ Trumpet* (1964).

7   *The Magnificent Seven* (1960) was modelled on what 1952 Japanese film?

8   What was John Ford's last western, made in 1964, starring Richard Widmark and Carroll Baker?

9   This 1965 movie starred Charlton Heston and Richard Harris, and was directed by Sam Peckinpah. Name it.

10   Who was Dirty Dingus Magee in the 1970 comedy western of the same name?

11   Name the two leads in *Little Big Man* (1970).

12   Who played Horse in *A Man Called Horse* (1970)?

13   Who starred in *A Man Called Sledge* (1970)?

14   Candice Bergen and Peter Strauss featured in what violent western of 1970?

15   Who were the two male leads in *The Wild Rovers* (1971)?

'Women are like elephants, they're good to look at but I wouldn't like to own one.'
– W.C. Fields

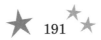

Answers

1. Jock Mahoney. The film starred James Stewart and Dean Martin

2. Roy Orbison

3. *Hang 'em High*

4. *El Dorado*

5. *Rancho Deluxe*

6. *A Distant Trumpet*

7. Akira Kurosawa's *The Seven Samurai*

8. *Cheyenne Autumn*

9. *Major Dundee*

10. Frank Sinatra

11. Dustin Hoffman and Faye Dunaway

12. Richard Harris

13. James Garner

14. *Soldier Blue*

15. William Holden and Ryan O'Neal

'Someone asked me would I like to play Hamlet? To hell with small towns,
I'll take New York.'
– Jimmy Durante

Take 3

1 Brad Pitt and Anthony Hopkins starred in what 1994 epic western?

2 Kevin Costner played a famous Wild West marshall in 1994. Name the film.

3 Walter Hill's *Geronimo: An American Legend* (1993) starred which two notable actors?

4 Oliver Hardy appeared in a John Wayne western of 1949. What was the movie called?

5 Who was Cat Ballou in the 1965 comedy western of the same name?

6 Who co-starred with Paul Newman in *Hombre* (1967) and had his own TV show *Have Gun Will Travel*?

7 Who played Jeremiah Johnson in the 1972 movie of the same title?

8 What cowboy cartoon character had his feature western in 1971?

9 Joan Crawford starred in a western in 1954. Name the movie.

10 What was Audie Murphy's last western in 1969 called?

11 Name the actor who played the marshall in *High Noon* (1952).

12 Who played John Wesley Hardin in *Lawless Breed* (1952)?

13 Name the 1957 movie that teamed James Stewart and Audie Murphy as brothers.

14 Sam Fuller's *Run of the Arrow* (1957) starred which actor?

15 What was the 1958 western with Gregory Peck, Jean Simmons, Charlton Heston and Carroll Baker?

'I went through it once but it was closed.'
– *W.C. Fields (on Philadelphia)*

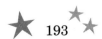

# nswers

1 *Legends of the Fall.* Henry Thomas and Aidan Quinn played Brad Pitt's brothers

2 *Wyatt Earp*

3 Gene Hackman and Robert Duvall

4 *The Fighting Kentuckian*

5 Jane Fonda

6 Richard Boone

7 Robert Redford

8 Lucky Luke. The movie of the same name was based on Goscinny's popular European comic strip with the voice of Richard Little

9 *Johnny Guitar*

10 *A Time for Dying*

11 Gary Cooper. The movie was directed by Fred Zinnemann

12 Rock Hudson

13 *Night Passage*

14 Rod Steiger

15 *The Big Country*, directed by William Wyler

'Listen, I've got three expressions –
looking left, looking right and looking straight ahead.'
– *Robert Mitchum (on acting)*

Take 4

1   Henry Fonda was Wyatt Earp, Victor Mature was Doc Holliday and John Ford directed. What was this classic 1946 western?

2   What was the 1946 musical western featuring Judy Garland, Ray Bolger and Angela Lansbury?

3   Name the male and female leads in *Dodge City* (1939).

4   Name the 1939 comedy western, starring James Stewart and Marlene Dietrich.

5   Who won an Oscar for his performance as Judge Roy Bean in *The Westerner* (1940)?

6   In 1981 Kris Kristofferson, Christopher Walken and John Hurt featured in what epic western that flopped at the box office?

7   Emilio Estevez, Kiefer Sutherland, Lou Diamond Phillips and Charlie Sheen starred in what 1988 western?

8   Which character actor was trying to catch a fly in his gun barrel at the beginning of *Once Upon a Time in The West* (1968)?

9   Name the character actor who was killed with a knife by James Coburn in *The Magnificent Seven* (1960).

10 What bit player actor went to Italy and became a star in such films as *For a few Dollars More* (1965), *The Good, the Bad and the Ugly* (1966) and *Barquero* (1970)?

11 *Cheyenne Social Club* (1970) starred James Stewart as a cowboy who inherited a brothel. Who directed this comedy western?

12 Singer Willie Nelson starred alongside Robert Redford and Jane Fonda in what contemporary western of 1979?

13 Spencer Tracy and Robert Young starred in what King Vidor western of 1940?

14 Which actor played a contemporary cowboy in *Lonely Are the Brave* (1962)?

15 Martin Sheen, Sam Waterston and Harvey Keitel starred in what 1978 western?

Answers

1. *My Darling Clementine*
2. *The Harvey Girls*
3. Errol Flynn and Olivia De Havilland
4. *Destry Rides Again*
5. Walter Brennan
6. Michael Cimino's *Heaven's Gate*
7. *Young Guns*
8. Jack Elam
9. Robert J. Wilkie
10. Lee Van Cleef
11. Gene Kelly
12. *The Electric Horseman*
13. *Northwest Passage*
14. Kirk Douglas
15. *Eagle's Wing*

'There's a hopeless poison that gets into actresses when they become big stars.'
– Kim Novak

Take 5

1   Who played Buffalo Bill in the 1944 movie of the same title?

2   This 1946 western, starring Gregory Peck and Jennifer Jones, was nicknamed *Lust in the Dust*. What was its real title?

3   *Silver Spurs* (1944) starred Roy Rogers. Who played his regular sidekick?

4   Who directed and starred in *The Alamo* (1960)?

5   Who featured in John Ford's courtroom drama western about a black cavalry man accused of rape?

6   Burt Lancaster, Audrey Hepburn and Audie Murphy starred in what 1960 western?

7   Complete the title of the John Wayne comedy western: *North to _____* (1960).

8   What was the last film for both Clark Gable and Marilyn Monroe?

9   Who played the gambler in *The Comancheros* (1961) and was arrested by Texas ranger John Wayne?

10 In the final scene of *The Last Sunset* (1961) he drew an empty gun on Rock Hudson. Can you name the actor?

11 Name the 1948 comedy western starring Bob Hope and Jane Russell.

12 What was the classic 1948 western by Howard Hawks starring John Wayne and Montgomery Clift?

13 Who starred as the Durango Kid in *Raiders of Tomahawk Creek* (1950)?

14 Name the 1950 John Ford western, starring Ben Johnson, Harry Carey Junior and Ward Bond.

15 What was the 1950 movie based on a story of a famous rifle, and starring James Stewart?

I am content with mediocrity.'
– *George Sanders*

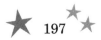

Answers

1   Joel McCrea. The movie also featured Maureen O'Hara

2   *Duel in the Sun*

3   Smiley Burnette

4   John Wayne (playing Davy Crockett)

5   Jeffery Hunter and Woody Strode

6   *The Unforgiven*, directed by John Huston

7   *North to Alaska.* The movie was directed by Henry Hathaway

8   *The Misfits* (1961), directed by John Huston

9   Stuart Whitman

10   Kirk Douglas

11   *The Paleface*

12   *Red River*

13   Charles Starrett, a popular B-movie star of the 1930s and 1940s.

14   *Wagon Master*

15   *Winchester '73*, directed by Anthony Mann

'If I have any genius in me, it's a genius for living.'
– Errol Flynn

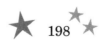

Take 6

1   Sidney Poitier and Harry Belafonte starred in what 1971 western?

2   Who played Liberty Valance in *The Man Who Shot Liberty Valance* (1962)?

3   Whose gold were Gregory Peck, Omar Sharif and Telly Savalas after in a movie from 1968?

4   Who played the crazed preacher in *Will Penny* (1967)?

5   Jim Brown and Raquel Welch starred in what western from 1969?

6   Complete the name of the 1971 film that was a rival to the Italian violent westerns and starred Robert Shaw and Martin Landau: *A Town Called* _____.

7   What was the 1963 comedy western featuring John Wayne and Maureen O'Hara?

8   Randolph Scott played Wyatt Earp in what western from 1939?

9   It won best picture and best director in the 1992 Academy Awards. What was the movie?

10   Complete the title of this Gregory Peck western from 1969: *The —— Moon*.

11   Name the hired gun in *Last of the Fast Guns* (1958).

12   Who played William 'Billy the Kid' Bonney in *Left Handed Gun* (1958)?

13   Who played the Pauite Indian on the run in *Tell Them Willie Boy Is Here* (1969)?

14   Singer Glen Campbell acted with John Wayne in what 1969 movie?

15   What 1966 western featured Pat Wayne (son of John) in a starring role?

Answers

1. *Buck and the Preacher*
2. Lee Marvin. The movie was directed by John Ford
3. McKenna's gold. Cllint Eastwood turned down the role that Gregory Peck played.
4. Donald Pleasence
5. *100 Rifles*
6. *A Town Called Bastard*
7. *McLintock*. The movie was directed by Andrew V. McLaglen
8. *Frontier Marshal*
9. *Unforgiven*, directed by Clint Eastwood
10. *The Stalking Moon*
11. Jock Mahoney
12. Paul Newman. The movie was directed by Arthur Penn
13. Robert Blake
14. *True Grit*
15. *An Eye for an Eye*

'If I'd stayed in Hollywood, I would have ended up
like Alan Ladd and Gail Russell – dead and buried by now.'
– *Veronica Lake*

Take 7

1   Peter Fonda and Warren Oates play two drifters in what 1971 movie?

2   Known as the singing cowboy with a horse called Trigger, name the top box office star from 1943 to 1954.

3   Another top box office star from 1936 to 1954, who had a horse named Champion, who was he?

4   *The Hour of the Gun* (1967) featured a story about Wyatt Earp and Doc Holliday. What actors played these roles?

5   Who played Chief Crazy Horse in the (1955) movie of the same title?

6   Who played Davy Crockett in *Davy Crockett: King of the Wild Frontier* (1955)?

7   Gary Cooper starred alongside Burt Lancaster in what 1954 western?

8   Which cowboy star was known as Hopalong Cassidy in the (1935) movie of the same title?

9   Which band provided the score for *Young Guns II: Blaze of Glory* (1990)?

10   Name the 1972 western in which Jeff Bridges and Barry Brown played draft dodgers in the old west.

11   Clark Gable, Jane Russell and Robert Ryan starred in what 1955 western, directed by Raoul Walsh?

12   What 1955 western starred Robert Wagner, Jeffrey Hunter and Debra Paget?

13   James Cagney replaced Spencer Tracy in what 1956 western?

14   Gregory Peck, Joan Collins and Stephen Boyd starred in what 1958 western?

15   Who starred in *Man of the West* (1958)?

'I don't want people to recognise me if I walk down the street.'
– *Robert De Niro*

Answers

1   *The Hired Hand*

2   Roy Rogers

3   Gene Autry

4   James Garner was Wyatt Earp and Jason Robards was Doc Holliday

5   Victor Mature. The movie is also known as *Valley of Fury*

6   Fess Parker

7   *Vera Cruz*

8   William Boyd

9   Bon Jovi

10 *Bad Company*

11 *The Tall Man*

12 *White Feather*

13 *Tribute to a Bad Man*

14 *The Bravados*

15 Gary Cooper

'His grin would melt stone.'
– New York critic (on Gene Kelly)

CINEMA GREATS

John Wayne

1   What was John Wayne's real name?

2   What was his nickname?

3   What was his first major movie, and in what year was the movie released?

4   What 1939 movie made him a star?

5   What was his character's name in *Stagecoach* (1939)?

6   Which famous singing cowboy co-starred with John Wayne in *Dark Command* (1940)?

7   Where was John Wayne born?

8   Name John Wayne's son, who appeared in several of his movies.

9   In what 1942 movie did Wayne have a classic fight scene with Randolph Scott?

10   Complete the title of the 1949 war movie starring John Wayne: *Flying* _____

11   Montgomery Clift played opposite Duke in what classic western from 1948?

12   Name the John Ford cavalry trilogy (1948, 1949, 1950) starring John Wayne.

13   In which of the above three movies did Henry Fonda appear?

14   Who played Maureen O'Hara's brother and had a public brawl with John Wayne in *The Quiet Man* (1952)?

15   Complete the title of this John Wayne war movie from 1949: *Sands of* _____ .

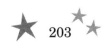

Answers

1 Marion Michael Morrison

2 Duke

3 *The Big Trail* (1930)

4 *Stage Coach*

5 The Ringo Kid

6 Roy Rogers

7 He was born in Winterset, Iowa on May 26 1907

8 Pat Wayne

9 *The Spoilers*

10 *Flying Leathernecks*

11 *Red River*

12 *Fort Apache, She Wore A Yellow Ribbon* and *Rio Grande*

13 *Fort Apache*

14 Victor McLaglen

15 *Sands of Iwo Jima*

John Wayne, the hero in many a movie about the American civil war, World War II
and the Vietnam war, in real life never served in the armed forces.

CINEMA GREATS

John Wayne

1   In what 1955 movie did John Wayne play Genghis Khan?

2   What was the name of John Wayne's character in *The Searchers* (1956)?

3   John Wayne and William Holden played opposite each other in what western from 1959?

4   John Wayne produced, directed and starred in what historical western drama of 1960?

5   Who played Sam Houston in the above movie?

6   A well-known pop idol of the late 1950s and early 1960s co-starred with John Wayne and Dean Martin in *Rio Bravo* (1959). Can you name him?

7   Name the 1959 comedy-western starring Duke, Stewart Granger and Capucine.

8   In *The Man Who Shot Liberty Valance* (1962), who played John Wayne's farmhand?

9   John Wayne's movies: *McLintock* (1963), *The Green Berets* (1968) and *Cahill: United States Marshal* (1973) were produced by his son. Can you name him?

10   In what all-star cast movie of 1965, about the life of Jesus, did Duke play a Roman soldier?

11   Name the 1962 movie about the D-Day landing, starring John Wayne and a host of stars, and based on a book by Cornelius Ryan.

12   What was John Wayne's last movie? In what year was it released?

13   Who played the doctor in the above movie?

14   John Wayne won an Oscar for what 1969 western?

15   In what year did Duke pass away?

Answers

1   *The Conqueror*

2   Nathan Hawke

3   *The Horse Soldiers*

4   *The Alamo*

5   Richard Boone

6   Ricky Nelson

7   *North To Alaska*

8   Woody Strode

9   Michael Wayne

10   *The Greatest Story Ever Told*

11   *The Longest Day*

12   *The Shootist* (1976)

13   James Stewart

14   *True Grit*

15   1979

'Her personality is limited. She's good as a peasant,
but incapable of playing a lady.'
– *Sophia Loren (on Gina Lollobrigida)*

COMEDY

Take 1

1   Mel Brooks directed what 1974 spoof western starring Gene Wilder and Cleavon Little?

2   Name the Gene Wilder/Zero Mostel classic comedy of 1967.

3   Name the gag-laden spoof disaster movie of 1980 starring Leslie Neilson.

4   Spencer Tracy, Mickey Rooney, Buster Keaton and The Three Stooges were among the all-star cast of what 1963 Stanley Kramer movie?

5   Marilyn Monroe proved how excellent a comic actor she was in *The Seven Year Itch* (1955). Can you name the director of the movie?

6   Victor Mature stole the movie from Peter Sellers in a send-up of his old Hollywood image. Name the 1966 movie.

7   Who was the original nutty professor from the 1963 film of the same title?

8   A classic Hollywood image from 1923 was the clock-hanging act in *Safety Last*. Who was the actor?

9   Complete the title of the Marx Brothers 1930 movie: *Animal* ____.

10 Name the hilarious policemen from the Mack Sennett silent comedies.

11 Her cuteness and talent made her the greatest child star in the depression of the 1930s. Appearing in such films of 1935 as *The Little Colonel* and *The Littlest Rebel*, can you name the girl?

12 Who, playing Andy, starred in the *Andy Hardy* series of movies?

13 Released in 1940, name the first movie the Marx Brothers starred in as a threesome – Groucho, Chico and Harpo.

14 What was Laurel and Hardy's first all-talking feature film of 1931?

15 What were the names of the Three Stooges?

'What is comedy? I don't know. Does anybody?'
– *Stan Laurel*

Answers

1   *Blazing Saddles*

2   *The Producers*, directed by Billy Wilder

3   *Airplane*

4   *It's a Mad, Mad, Mad, Mad World*

5   Billy Wilder

6   *After the Fox*, directed by Vittorio De Sica

7   Jerry Lewis

8   Harold Lloyd

9   *Animal Crackers*

10   The Keystone Cops

11.   Shirley Temple

12   Mickey Rooney

13   *Go West*

14   *Pardon Us*, directed by Hal Roach

15   Moe, Larry and Curley – originally Moe Howard, Larry Fine and Shemp Howard (who left and was replaced by his brother Curley)

'My acting career has nothing to do with my sexuality,
I was gay last year, I'm gay this year and I'll be gay next year.'
– *Rupert Everett*

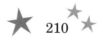

Take 2

1   Name the film that shot Michael Caine to international fame in 1966.

2   Name the nine most regular stars of the *Carry On* team.

3   In what year was *The Life of Brian* made: 1970, 1979 or 1983?

4   What was the first *The Road to . . .* movie in 1940, starring Bing Crosby, Dorothy Lamour and Bob Hope?

5   Who were 'the odd couple' in the 1968 movie of the same name?

6   Who played Inspector Clouseau in the *Pink Panther* movies?

7   Who was the lead star in *Private Benjamin* (1980)?

8   What movie paired Ryan O'Neal and Barbra Streisand in 1972?

9   Complete the title of the 1949 comedy starring Bob Hope: —— *Jones.*

10 Who directed *National Lampoon's Animal House* (1978)?

11 Who played Mary in the Farrelly brothers' *There's Something About Mary* (1998)?

12 Who played the love interest in *Shallow Hal* (2001), starring Jack Black?

13 Kevin Spacey starred in what highly successful black comedy of 2000, directed by Sam Mendes?

14 Jackie Gleeson and Burt Reynolds starred in what popular comedy of 1977?

15 In what *Carry On* movie of 1967 did American actor Phil Silvers star?

Despite popular belief, Alan Ladd was not the smallest leading man. He was 5'6", one inch taller than Dustin Hoffman, and the same height as Al Pacino. The smallest actor is Verne Troyer. He played Mini Me in *Austin Powers, The Spy Who Shagged Me* (1999).

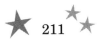

Answers

1   *Alfie*. The movie also starred Vivien Merchant, Shelley Winters and Jane Asher

2   Sid James, Kenneth Williams, Kenneth Connor, Jim Dale, Hattie Jacques, Joan Sims, Bernard Breslaw, Barbara Windsor and Charles Hawtrey

3   1979

4   *The Road to Singapore*

5   Jack Lemmon and Walter Matthau. The movie was adapted from a Neil Simon play

6   Peter Sellers, except for one film in which Alan Arkin played the role. Steve Martin will play Clouseau in 2005

7   Goldie Hawn

8   *What's Up, Doc?*

9   *Sorrowful Jones*. The movie also starred Lucille Ball

10 John Landis

11 Cameron Diaz

12 Gwyneth Paltrow

13. *American Beauty*

14 *Smokey and the Bandit*

15 *Carry On Follow that Camel*

'There are two parts to film: making it and selling it.'
– William Goldman

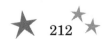

Take 3

1   Name the wacky, tuneful 1964 parody of *The Man from Sherwood*, starring Frank Sinatra, Dean Martin, Bing Crosby and Sammy Davis Junior.

2   Woody Allen took advice from Bogart on handling women in what 1972 comedy?

3   What was the classic comedy from 1959 starring Tony Curtis, Jack Lemmon and Marilyn Monroe?

4   Who played the gentleman cat burglar in *The Pink Panther* (1963)?

5   Name the classic Disney short from 1937 with Mickey Mouse, Goofy and Donald Duck.

6   The Marx Brothers only made 13 movies together. What was their famous 1946 spoof on the Humphrey Bogart classic of 1942?

7   The Laurel and Hardy International Fan Club took its name from what Stan and Ollie movie of 1933?

8   Name the two leads in *The Owl and the Pussycat* (1970)?

9   This 1997 comic twist on Tarzan had Brendan Fraser getting advice on how to woo a woman from ape John Cleese. Name the movie.

10 Name the 1937 movie in which the great comedy duo Laurel and Hardy sing 'On the Trail of the Lonesome Pine'.

11 Name the Abbott and Costello movie of 1948 where Bela Lugosi turns up as Dracula.

12 It was W.C. Fields last starring movie in 1941. Can you name it?

13 What was the comedy from 1965 starring Peter O'Toole, Peter Sellers, Woody Allen and Ursula Andress?

14 In the 2001 remake of *Around the World in 80 Days* which martial arts star played the comic sidekick?

15 Robert Redford and Jane Fonda starred in what romantic comedy from 1967?

Answers

1   *Robin and the Seven Hoods*

2   *Play It Again, Sam*, directed by Herbert Ross

3   *Some Like It Hot*, directed by Billy Wilder

4   David Niven. The movie was directed by Blake Edwards

5   *The Clock Cleaners*

6   *A Night in Casablanca*

7   *Sons of the Desert*

8   Barbra Streisand and George Segal

9   *George of the Jungle*

10   *Way out West*

11   *Abbott and Costello Meet Frankenstein*

12   *Never Give a Sucker an Even Break*

13   *What's New Pussycat*

14   Jackie Chan

15   *Barefoot in the Park*

'We'd try one thing – it wasn't funny; we'd try something else.'
– *Hal Roach*

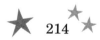

Take 4

1   Who starred in the Ealing comedy *Lavender Hill Mob* (1951)?

2   Who was the personnel man in the Boulting Brothers' *I'm All Right Jack* (1959)?

3   Kenneth More and Kay Kendall starred in what 1953 film about a veteran car race from London to Brighton?

4   How many roles did Peter Sellers play in *Dr. Strangelove, or How I Learned to Stop Worrying and Love the Bomb* (1963)?

5   Who played Tom Jones in the 1963 movie of the same name?

6   French comedian Fernandel had his greatest success as the priest in what 1952 movie?

7   Who starred in the comedy *No Time for Sergeants* (1958)?

8   Clark Gable and Claudette Colbert starred in what Frank Capra movie of 1934?

9   In what comedy of 1944 did Bing Crosby win an Oscar for his role as a priest?

10   Diane Keaton won an Academy Award for what 1977 movie, co-starring Woody Allen, who also directed?

11   Rock Hudson and Doris Day starred in what glossy comedy from 1964?

12   Cary Grant starred in what 1964 black comedy directed by Frank Capra?

13   Bill Murray and Dan Aykroyd starred in what highly successful supernatural comedy of 1984?

14   Name the popular Dustin Hoffman movie of 1982 about an out-of-work actor who dressed up as a woman to get work.

15   Who played a petty New York conman in *Trading Places* (1983)?

'I love being Black in America and especially being Black in Hollywood.'
– *Will Smith*

Answers

1. Alec Guinness and Stanley Holloway
2. Terry Thomas
3. *Genevieve*
4. Three: An airman, the president and a US Nazi advisor
5. Albert Finney. The movie was directed by Tony Richardson
6. *The Little World of Don Camillo*
7. Andy Griffith
8. *It Happened One Night*
9. *Going My Way*
10. *Annie Hall*
11. *Send Me No Flowers*
12. *Arsenic and Old Lace*
13. *Ghostbusters*
14. *Tootsie*
15. Eddie Murphy

'I can meet a Nobel Prize winning physicist and he'll say:
"You're Mork aren't you? How's Mindy?"'
– *Robin Williams*

WAR

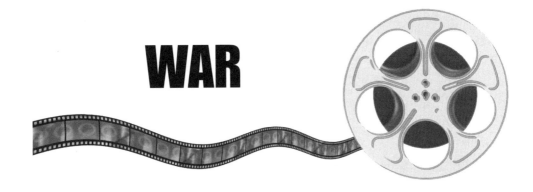

Take 1

1 Who won an Academy Award for his performance in *The Bridge on the River Kwai* (1957)?

2 Name the 1958 movie in which Ingrid Bergman starred as an English missionary in war time.

3 Name the 1961 movie about Nazi war crimes, starring Spencer Tracy as the judge.

4 Can you name the six male leads in *The Guns of Navarone* (1961), directed by J. Lee Thompson.

5 Who played the lead role as Major Falconer in Sydney Pollack's *Castle Keep* (1969)?

6 Roger Corman directed a 1964 war movie starring Stewart Granger and Mickey Rooney. Can you name it?

7 In what 1966 movie, directed by Robert Aldrich and starring Lee Marvin, was a team of dangerous criminals assigned to a hazardous mission?

8 Kirk Douglas and John Wayne starred in what Otto Preminger movie from 1965?

9 Name the 1961 film based on Willis Hall's play and starring Laurence Harvey, Richard Todd and Richard Harris.

10 Can you name the 1964 film based on the trial of a deserter during World War I, starring Dirk Bogarde?

11 John Lennon starred in what black comedy from 1967 directed by Richard Lester?

12 Frank Sinatra and Tony Curtis starred in what war movie from 1958?

13 On board the HMS *Ajax* ready to do battle were Anthony Quayle and Patrick MacNee. Name the 1956 movie.

14 'There's still time, brother!' The final ironic message from what 1959 movie in which Gregory Peck, Ava Gardner and Fred Astaire await death by nuclear fall-out?

15 Who played Yossarian in Joseph Heller's *Catch 22* (1970)?

Answers

1   Alec Guinness. The movie was directed by David Lean

2   *The Inn of the Sixth Happiness*

3   *Judgement at Nuremberg*, directed by Stanley Kramer

4   Gregory Peck, David Niven, Anthony Quinn, James Darren, Stanley Baker and Anthony Quayle

5   Burt Lancaster

6   *The Secret Invasion*

7   *The Dirty Dozen*

8   *In Harm's Way*

9   *The Long and the Short and the Tall*

10 *King and Country*, directed by Joseph Losey

11 *How I Won the War*

12 *Kings Go Forth*

13 *The Battle of River Plate*

14 *On the Beach*, directed by Stanley Kramer

15 Alan Arkin. The movie was directed by Mike Nichols

'Great double acts are extremely rare, it's a million to one chance that two people
can get together. This miracle happens, it happened with Laurel and Hardy.'
– *Ernie Wise*

Take 2

1   Richard Burton and Clint Eastwood starred in this 1968 film, which was inspired by an Alistair MacLean novel. What was the film?

2   Burt Lancaster played a railway engineer in *The Train* (1964), directed by John Frankenheimer. Who played the German officer?

3   Who starred as Captain Queeg in *The Caine Mutiny* (1954)?

4   Who was the reluctant soldier-hero Sergeant York in the 1941 movie of the same title, directed by Howard Hawks?

5   Who starred in *The Great Dictator* (1940)?

6   Complete the title of the 1940 James Cagney movie: *The Fighting _____.*

7   Who played the lead in *Gung Ho* (1944)?

8   Who were the rival submarine officers in *Run Silent, Run Deep* (1958)?

9   Audie Murphy, the most decorated soldier of World War II, played himself in what movie of 1955?

10   What was the Don Siegel movie of 1962 starring Steve McQueen?

11   Name the 1953 film that dealt with the Korean War and starred Victor Mature, Lee Marvin and Richard Egan?

12   Who played the lead in *Objective Burma* (1945), directed by Raoul Walsh?

13   Peter O'Toole and Omar Sharif were teamed again in what movie from 1966?

14   Who was the Russian sniper in *Enemy at the Gates* (2001)?

15   *Carve Her Name With Pride* (1958) was the story of Violette Szabo, a resistance worker. Who played her?

The Vietnamese village sets built for *The Green Berets* (1970) in Fort Benning Georgia in 1967 were so realistic that the US army used them for training troops before shipping them to Vietnam.

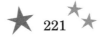

Answers

1   *Where Eagles Dare*

2   Paul Scofield

3   Humphrey Bogart. The movie was directed by Edward Dmytryk

4   Gary Cooper

5   Charlie Chaplin, who also directed the movie

6   *The Fighting 69th*

7   Randolph Scott

8   Clark Gable and Burt Lancaster. The movie was directed by Robert Wise

9   *To Hell and Back*

10   *Hell Is for Heroes*

11   *The Glory Brigade.* The Korean war ended a month after this film was released

12   Errol Flynn

13   *The Night of the Generals*

14   Jude Law

15   Virginia McKenna

In the movie *The Big Red One* (1980), all the Nazi guards in the concentration camp were played by Jews.

Take 3

1   Directed by John Huston and Mervyn LeRoy, this 1955 movie starred Henry Fonda, James Cagney, William Powell and Jack Lemmon. Name it.

2   Based on a novel by Leon Uris, what 1960 film starred Paul Newman, John Derek, Ralph Richardson and Eva Marie Saint?

3   What aquatic war drama from 1951 starred Richard Widmark, Dana Andrews and Jeffery Hunter?

4   Name Carl Foreman's anti-war movie of 1963, starring George Peppard, George Hamilton and Jeanne Moreau.

5   In the movie *No Time to Die* (1958), Victor Mature co-starred with which comic british actor?

6   Who directed the all-star cast in *A Bridge Too Far* (1977)?

7   Who starred with Robert Stack in *The High and the Mighty* (1954)?

8   Who directed the four times Oscar winner *Platoon* (1986)?

9   Tom Hanks starred and Steven Spielberg directed. What was the Oscar-winning movie of 1998?

10 Name Francis Ford Coppola's epic Vietnam movie of 1979, starring Marlon Brando and Martin Sheen.

11 What 1958 film, based on a Norman Mailer novel and starring Ray Aldo, did Raoul Walsh direct?

12 Complete the title: *The Battle of _____ _____* (1965), starring Henry Fonda and Robert Shaw.

13 The Queen of England's favourite actor starred in *Sink the Bismarck!* (1960). Can you name him?

14 How many directors worked on *Tora, Tora, Tora* (1970)?

15 Who won the Best Supporting Actor Oscar for *The Deer Hunter* (1978)?

Answers

1 *Mister Roberts*

2 *Exodus*, directed by Otto Preminger

3 *The Frogmen*

4 *The Victors*

5 Anthony Newley

6 Richard Attenborough

7 John Wayne

8 Oliver Stone

9 *Saving Private Ryan*

10 *Apocalypse Now*

11 *The Naked and the Dead*

12 *The Battle of the Bulge*

13 Kenneth More

14 Three: Richard Fleischer, Toshio Masuda and Kinji Fukasaku

15 Christopher Walken

'Chaplin was the greatest.'
– *Stan Laurel*

Take 4

1 Charlton Heston and Henry Fonda starred in what 1976 sea battle movie?

2 Who played Hitler in *The Last Ten Days* (1973)?

3 Name the John Boorman movie of 1969 starring Lee Marvin and Toshiro Mifune.

4 John Wayne directed and starred in what Vietnam movie in 1968?

5 Complete the 1950 film title: *The Halls of* _____, in which Robert Wagner made his screen debut.

6 What 1958 film starred Richard Attenborough and John Mills?

7 Who played the two leads in *The Dambusters* (1954)?

8 What duo starred in the 1943 comedy *Air Raid Wardens*?

9 Cornel Wilde directed and starred in what movie of 1967?

10 Name the 1966 movie in which George Peppard played an ace German pilot.

11 Who directed the 1998 version of *The Thin Red Line*?

12 Name the two leads in *The Colditz Story* (1954)?

13 Who starred in *The Forty-Ninth Parallel* (1941)?

14 Sam Fuller directed it, but can you name the leads in *The Big Red One* (1980)?

15 When was *All Quiet on the Western Front* made: 1927, 1930 or 1933?

'Stan was the greatest, Chaplin was second.'
– Buster Keaton

Answers

1   *Midway*

2   Alec Guinness

3   *Hell in the Pacific*

4   *The Green Berets*

5   *The Halls of Montezuma*

6   *Dunkirk*

7   Michael Redgrave and Richard Todd

8   Laurel and Hardy

9   *Beach Red*

10   *The Blue Max*

11   Terence Malick

12   John Mills and Eric Portman

13   Laurence Olivier and Eric Portman

14   Lee Marvin and Mark Hamill

15   1930. The movie was based on a novel by Erich Maria Remarque

'I was doing any movie I could just to get practice.'
– *Sir Ian McKellen (on his early career)*

Take 5

1   Directed by and starring Frank Sinatra, what was this 1965 movie?

2   Laurence Olivier played Chief Marshall Sir Hugh Dowding in what all-star cast movie of 1969?

3   James Garner, Steve McQueen, James Coburn and Donald Pleasence starred in what POW drama of 1962?

4   William Holden won an Oscar for his performance in what 1953 movie directed by Billy Wilder?

5   George Segal and Tom Courtenay starred in what 1965 movie?

6   Name the Robert Aldrich 1956 war drama, starring Jack Palance, Eddie Albert and Lee Marvin.

7   Name the 2001 film about code-breakers in World War II.

8   Which director won the Cannes Award for *M*A*S*H* (1969)?

9   Who played General Douglas MacArthur in *MacArthur* (1970)?

10   Who played JFK in *PT 109* (1963)?

11   It was directed by Arthur Hiller and starred Rock Hudson and George Peppard. Name the desert action movie of 1967.

12   Who starred in *Murphy's War* (1970), directed by Peter Yates?

13   Gore Vidal and Francis Ford Coppola were two of the screenwriters on what all-star, multingual war drama from 1966?

14   Robert Wise directed what 1966 movie starring Steve McQueen and Richard Attenborough?

15   *The One That Got Away* (1957) starred which German actor?

Hitler ordered Josef Goebbels, the Third Reich censor, to insist that in any movie where a woman broke up a marriage, that woman must die before the movie ended.

Answers

1   *None But the Brave*. The movie also starred Clint Walker

2   *The Battle of Britain*

3   *The Great Escape*, directed by John Sturges

4   *Stalag 17*

5   *King Rat*, directed Bryan Forbes

6   *Attack!*

7   *Enigma*

8   Robert Altman

9   Gregory Peck

10   Cliff Robertson

11   *Tobruk*

12   Peter O'Toole

13   *Is Paris Burning?*

14   *The Sand Pebbles*

15   Hardy Kruger

In *The Great Escape* (1963) Steve McQueen escaped on a motorbike and was chased by a German on another bike. In reality, it was Steve McQueen doing both stunts. He was chasing himself! The magic of movie making . . .

EPICS

Take 1

1. Tony Curtis was one-handed and Kirk Douglas ended up with one eye. Can you name the epic movie of 1958?

2. *55 Days at Peking* was about the Boxer Rebellion of 1900. Who were the three stars in this 1963 movie?

3. In what year was *Gone With the Wind* made: 1935, 1939 or 1942?

4. Rod Steiger played Napoleon in *Waterloo* (1970). Who played Wellington?

5. Richard Widmark played a Viking and Sidney Poitier played a Moorish prince in what 1963 epic adventure?

6. Who portrayed Alexander in *Alexander the Great* (1956)?

7. Who played General George Custer in *Custer of the West* (1968)?

8. Who was Hannibal in the 1959 movie of the same name?

9. Yul Brynner and Tony Curtis starred as Cossack father and son in what sixteenth century epic from 1962?

10. Who played Lara in *Doctor Zhivago* (1965), directed by David Lean?

11. Who portrayed the legendary Lawrence in *Lawrence of Arabia* (1962)?

12. What 1980 film was made about the Boer War and starred Edward Woodward?

13. What was the 1962 western epic with an all-star cast and employing the three-camera cinerama technique?

14. Name the 1964 movie, directed by Cy Enfield, starring Stanley Baker and Michael Caine.

15. What was the classic Errol Flynn western epic of 1941, directed by Raoul Walsh?

Answers

1   *The Vikings*, directed by Richard Fleischer

2   Charlton Heston, Ava Gardner and David Niven

3   1939. The movie starred Clark Gable and Vivien Leigh

4   Christopher Plummer

5   *The Long Ships*

6   Richard Burton

7   Robert Shaw

8   Victor Mature

9   *Tarus Bulba*

10   Julie Christie. Omar Sharif was Zhivago

11   Peter O'Toole

12   *Breaker Morant*

13   *How The West Was Won*

14   *Zulu*

15   *They Died With Their Boots On*. The movie also starred Olivia De Havilland and Arthur Kennedy

'I will never do another movie when the people are alive.'
– *William Goldman (on writing* A Bridge Too Far *about WWII heroics)*

Take 2

1   Who played Jesus in *The Greatest Story Ever Told* (1965)?

2   Anthony Quinn played the role of the thief who was released from prison while Christ was crucified in his place. Name the movie.

3   In *King of Kings* (1961) who played Pontius Pilate?

4   Who played Hercules in the 1957 movie of the same name?

5   What was the first genuine epic in cinema history, made by D.W. Griffith and released in 1915?

6   Who made *The Ten Commandments* in 1923 and again in 1956?

7   In *The Abdication* (1973), who played Queen Christina of Sweden?

8   Name Eisenstein's great epic from 1925 about the universal struggle against oppression?

9   Who played Captain Bligh in the 1935 version of *Mutiny on the Bounty*?

10 Who starred in the epic *Prince of Foxes* (1949)?

11 When was the classic silent film *Napoleon* made: 1920, 1925 or 1927?

12 *Quo Vadis* (1951), directed by Mervyn LeRoy, starred Robert Taylor and Deborah Kerr as the lovers. Who played Nero?

13 Who played Nicholas and Alexandra in the 1971 film of the same title?

14 Who played Jesus in *The Last Temptation of Christ* (1988)?

15 Who played Queen Elizabeth I in the historical drama *The Virgin Queen* (1955)?

In the movie *Helen Of Troy* (1955), an aeroplane passes overhead in one scene!

# Answers

1   Max Von Sydow

2   *Barabbas*, directed by Richard Fleischer

3   Hurd Hatfield (of Dorian Gray fame)

4   Steve Reeves

5   *The Birth of a Nation*, based on Thomas Dixon's *The Clansman*

6   Cecil B. DeMille

7   Liv Ullmann. The movie also starred Peter Finch and Cyril Cusack

8   *The Battleship Potemkin*. The movie was banned in France until 1953 due to political censorship

9   Charles Laughton

10   Tyrone Power

11   1927. The movie was directed by Abel Gance

12   Peter Ustinov

13   Michael Jayston and Janet Suzman

14   Willem Dafoe. The movie was directed by Martin Scorsese

15   Bette Davis

'My co-stars are really impressive. I know that if *Jurassic Park III* (fails), it's the dinosaurs' fault.'
– *Tea Leoni*

Take 3

1   Name the four leads in *The English Patient* (1997)?

2   What was the Bernardo Bertolucci epic of 1987, set in China, and starring John Lone, Joan Chen and Peter O'Toole?

3   Complete the title of this 1971 movie with Michael Caine and Omar Sharif: *The _____ Valley.*

4   Who played Zeus in *Clash of the Titans* (1981)?

5   Who played Hecuba in *The Trojan Women* (1971), directed by Michael Cacoyannis?

6   What 1959 Tarzan movie saw Sean Connery as a bad guy?

7   Elizabeth Taylor was Cleopatra, Richard Burton was Marc Antony, but who played Julius Caesar in the 1963 epic *Cleopatra*?

8   Released in 1981, name the first of the Indiana Jones trilogy, starring Harrison Ford?

9   Who played the doomed lovers in *Titanic* (1997)?

10 In what 1997 movie did Leonardo DiCaprio play a dual role?

11 Paul Scofield won an Oscar for *A Man for all Seasons* (1966), playing Sir Thomas Moore. Who played King Henry VIII?

12 What was the 1962 safari romp filmed in East Africa and starring John Wayne, Elsa Martinelli and Hardy Kruger?

13 Can you name the two stars of *Sons of the Musketeers* (1951)?

14 Who starred as Cleopatra in the 1945 film version of George Bernard Shaw's play Caesar and Cleopatra?

15 Sophia Loren, Stephen Boyd, Alec Guinness, Christopher Plummer and James Mason starred in what historical epic of 1964?

Actor Jon Hall suffered real whipping, carried heavy loads in the blazing sun, and fought a real shark in *Hurricane* (1937). All for art!

Answers

1   Ralph Fiennes, Kristin Scott Thomas, Juliette Binoche and Willem Dafoe

2   *The Last Emperor*

3   *The Last Valley*

4   Laurence Olivier

5   Katharine Hepburn

6   *Tarzan's Greatest Adventure*, starring Gordon Scott as Tarzan

7   Rex Harrison

8   *Raiders of the Lost Ark*, directed by Steven Spielberg

9   Leonardo DiCaprio and Kate Winslet

10 *The Man With the Iron Mask*

11 Robert Shaw. The movie was directed by Fred Zinnemann

12 *Hatari*, directed by Howard Hawks

13 Cornel Wilde and Maureen O'Hara

14 Vivien Leigh

15 *The Fall of the Roman Empire*, directed by Anthony Mann

Indiana Jones was the real name of George Lucas's dog.

Take 4

1   What was the first cinemascope movie in 1953, starring Richard Burton, Jean Simmons, Victor Mature and Michael Rennie?

2   King Vidor directed Tolstoy's *War and Peace* (1956). Name the three leading stars.

3   Complete the title of this 1962 movie: *The _____ Spartans*.

4   Name the four leading stars of *Beau Geste* (1939).

5   When was the classic movie *Casablanca* made: 1939, 1940 or 1942?

6   Who played Constantine in *Constantine and the Cross* (1963)?

7   Who played Salome to Charles Laughton's King Herod in *Salome* (1953)?

8   Name the sequel to *The Robe* (1953), starring Victor Mature, Susan Hayward and Michael Rennie.

9   Who played Marcus Aurelius in *Gladiator* (2000)?

10 Which comic actor appeared in *The Last Samurai* (2003)?

11 Who played the heroic explorer Robert Falcon Scott in *Scott of the Antarctic* (1948)?

12 Who starred in the classic swashbuckling adventure *The Sea Hawk* (1940)?

13 What 1981 movie recalls the clash between Native Americans and Jesuits of the seventeenth century?

14 Can you name Stanley Kubrick's 1975 Georgian odyssey set in 1789?

15 Richard Burton and Victor Mature palyed lead roles in *The Robe* (1953), but which actors were cast for their parts originally?

'I think violence in the movies gets a bad rap. "They saw this film and it made them want to go out and shoot people." Bullshit.'
– *Mel Gibson (on his film* Payback)

Answers

1 *The Robe*

2 Henry Fonda, Audrey Hepburn and Mel Ferrer

3 *The 300 Spartans*, starring Richard Egan and Ralph Richardson

4 Gary Cooper, Ray Milland, Robert Preston and Brian Donlevy

5 1942. The movie was directed by Michael Curtis and starred Humphrey Bogart, Ingrid Bergman and Claude Rains

6 Cornel Wilde

7 Rita Hayworth

8 *Demetrius and the Gladiators* (1954), directed by Delmer Davis

9 Richard Harris. The movie was directed by Ridley Scott

10 Billy Connolly. The movie starred Tom Cruise

11 John Mills. The movie was directed by Charles Frend

12 Errol Flynn. The movie was directed by Michael Curtiz

13 *The Black Robe*

14 *Barry Lyndon*, starring Ryan O'Neal and Hardy Kruger

15 Tyrone Power and Burt Lancaster

'Kubrick's work has often been described as cold and detached.
And Steven is just the opposite.'
– *Kathleen Kennedy (on Spielberg's direction of* A.I.*)*

THRILLERS

Take 1

1. Kevin Costner played Eliot Ness the US Treasury agent, in what Brian De Palma film from 1982?

2. Sergio Leone's final movie from 1984 starred Robert De Niro and James Woods. What was it called?

3. Who directed and starred in *A Perfect World* (1993)?

4. John Travolta and Samuel L. Jackson starred in what crime thriller from 1994?

5. A surfing dude goes undercover to infiltrate a gang suspected of robbing banks. Starring Patrick Swayze and Keanu Reeves, name this 1991 film.

6. Name the John Boorman movie from 1967, starring Lee Marvin and Angie Dickenson.

7. What was the classy spy thriller from Alfred Hitchcock made in 1959 and starring Cary Grant, Eva Marie Saint and James Mason?

8. Name the thriller from 1985, set in England with Gabriel Byrne, Denholm Elliot and Greta Scacchi.

9. Paul Newman consumed a vast quantity of hard-boiled eggs in one scene of this classic prison drama of 1967. What was it called?

10. Clint Eastwood moved away from the western but still wore a cowboy hat in this crime thriller from 1968. Name the movie.

11. Gene Hackman played a lonely surveillance expert in what movie of 1974?

12. It was the first of the spin-offs from the hugely successful TV spy show *The Man From U.N.C.L.E.*. Can you name this 1968 movie?

13. Robert De Niro portrayed a Vietnam veteran and his slow descent into hell trying to save a child prostitute. Name this 1976 film.

14. Name Alan Parker's tense thriller of 1987 set in New Orleans, starring Mickey Rourke as a New York private detective on the trail of a missing person.

15. This 1975 movie dealt with the dark side of politics in the wake of Watergate. Starring Robert Redford, Faye Dunaway, Cliff Robertson and Max Von Sydow, what was it called?

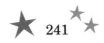

Answers

1   *The Untouchables.*. Robert De Niro was Al Capone and Sean Connery was Malone

2   *Once Upon a Time in America*

3   Clint Eastwood. The movie also starred Kevin Costner and Laura Dern

4   *Pulp Fiction.* Directed by Quentin Tarantino, the movie also starred Bruce Willis and Uma Thurman

5   *Point Break.* The movie also starred Gary Busey

6   *Point Blank.* This was Boorman's first time to direct an American production

7   *North by Northwest*

8   *Defence of the Realm*

9   *Cool Hand Luke.* Jack Lemmon's production company made this film

10 *Coogan's Bluff.* Directed by Don Siegel, the movie also starred Lee J. Cobb

11 *The Conversation,* directed by Francis Ford Coppola

12 *To Trap a Spy.* The movie starred Robert Vaughn and David McCallum

13 *Taxi Driver,* directed by Martin Scorsese

14 *Angel Heart.* The movie also starred Robert De Niro

15 *Three Days of the Condor,* directed by Sidney Pollack

'I've done my bit for movies, I stopped making them.'
– Liberace

Take 2

1 Who starred in *King of New York* (1989)?

2 Pierce Brosnan played a dastardly Russian spy, with Michael Caine as the British agent on his trail. Name the 1987 movie.

3 Name the 1991 movie in which Dustin Hoffman was the mobster and Nicole Kidman his moll.

4 Humphrey Bogart played Philip Marlowe in what film noir classic of 1946?

5 It was a top thriller from 1948, starring Victor Mature, Richard Conte and Shelly Winters. Complete the title: *Cry of _____ _____* .

6 Who played Dillinger in the 1973 movie of the same title?

7 Who starred in *Death Wish* (1974) and its four sequels?

8 Who was the leading male in *The FBI Story* (1959)?

9 Gloria Grahame gets her face scalded by coffee hurled at her by villain Lee Marvin. Can you name the film noir from 1953?

10 Name the male and female leads in the sizzling crime thriller *The Big Easy* (1986)?

11 James Stewart starred as an investigative reporter trying to clear Richard Conte of a murder rap. Name this crime drama from 1948.

12 Burt Lancaster and Shelley Winters starred in what gritty thriller from 1961?

13 Who starred in *The Wrong Man* (1956), directed by Alfred Hitchcock?

14 Name the martial arts action movie from 1973, starring Bruce Lee and John Saxon.

15 Al Pacino played a Puerto Rican hoodlum and Sean Penn played his lawyer. Can you name the 1993 movie?

One of America's most notorious gangsters John Dillinger was shot dead in 1934, but no movie was allowed to be made about him for over ten years, by order of the Hays Office in the USA.

Answers

1   Christopher Walken. The movie was directed by Abel Ferrara

2   *The Fourth Protocol*

3   *Billy Bathgate*

4   *The Big Sleep*. The movie, directed by Howard Hawks, also starred Lauren Bacall

5   *Cry of the City*, directed by Robert Siodmak

6   Warren Oates. The movie also starred Ben Johnson

7   Charles Bronson. The movie was directed by Michael Winner

8   James Stewart. The movie also starred Vera Miles

9   *The Big Heat* (1953). Directed by Fritz Lang, the movie also starred Glenn Ford

10 Dennis Quaid and Ellen Barkin

11 *Call Northside 777*

12 *The Young Savages*

13 Henry Fonda and Vera Miles

14 *Enter the Dragon*. This was Bruce Lee at his brilliant best, and sadly was his last completed movie

15 *Carlito's Way*

Scarface (1983) set in the Miami of 1980, showed *USA Today* for sale in the streets. The magazine did not come out until 1982!

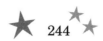

Take 3

1 Richard Gere played the lawyer defending altar boy Edward Norton in what 1996 thriller?

2 Al Pacino played the New York mayor in what 1996 political thriller?

3 This 1991 movie showed a brutal and candid view of Los Angeles street life and starred Laurence Fishburne, Cuba Gooding Junior and rapper Ice Cube. Can you name it?

4 Robert Walker and Farley Granger starred in what 1951 Hitchcock movie?

5 Who directed and starred in the classic film noir *Touch of Evil* (1958)?

6 Who directed *Chinatown* (1974)?

7 Mickey Rourke was top cop clearing up Chinatown of its villains in what 1985 movie?

8 Robert Mitchum got caught up in the Japanese underworld in what movie from 1975?

9 Who won an Oscar for his portrayal of a gay prisoner in *Kiss of the Spider Woman* (1986)?

10 Name the private detective played by Humphrey Bogart in the classic movie *The Maltese Falcon* (1941).

11 A stellar cast including Robert De Niro, Kevin Bacon, Dustin Hoffman, Brad Pitt and Jason Patric starred in what 1996 movie?

12 The Coen Brothers' prohibition gangster saga of 1990 starred Gabriel Byrne and Albert Finney. Name the movie.

13 Name the runaway success from 1991 written and directed by Quentin Tarantino.

14 Bridget Fonda and Jennifer Jason Leigh starred in what 1992 thriller about a roommate from hell?

15 Gregory Peck, Laurence Olivier and James Mason starred in what 1978 movie about cloning Hitler's body tissue to create identical boys who would help revive the Third Reich?

Answers

1 *Primal Fear*

2 *City Hall*. The movie also starred John Cusack and Bridget Fonda

3 *Boyz 'n the Hood* (1991), written and directed by John Singleton, when he was twenty-three

4 *Stranger on a Train*

5 Orson Welles. The movie also starred Charlton Heston and Janet Leigh

6 Roman Polanski. The movie starred Jack Nicholson and Faye Dunaway

7 *Year of the Dragon*, directed by Michael Cimino

8 *The Yakuza*, directed by Sidney Pollack

9 William Hurt

10 Sam Spade

11 *Sleepers*

12 *Miller's Crossing*, directed by Joel Coen

13 *Reservoir Dogs*. The film was Tarantino's directorial debut

14 *Single White Female*

15 *The Boys From Brazil*, directed by Franklin J. Shaffner

'Well at least he has finally found his true love
– what a pity he can't marry himself.'
– *Frank Sinatra (on Robert Redford)*

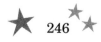

Take 4

1 In *Die Hard With a Vengeance* (1995) who played the villainous bomber with a desire for gold?

2 What was David Lynch's psychological thriller from 1996, starring Bill Pullman, Patricia Arquette and Robert Loggia?

3 Who played Al Capone in the 1959 movie of the same title?

4 It was a disaster movie from 1970, based on an Arthur Hailey novel, which went on to spawn three sequels. Name it.

5 Jodie Foster and Anthony Hopkins starred in what psychological thriller from 1991?

6 Kirk Douglas, Burt Lancaster and Wenden Corey starred in what thriller from 1947?

7 Based on a John Grisham novel, can you name the 1993 movie in which Tom Cruise was a rising young lawyer?

8 Michael Winner directed *Fire Power* in 1979. Can you name the stars?

9 John Huston directed this exceptional film noir in 1950, starring Sterling Hayden. Can you name the movie?

10 Name the two leads in *Atlantic City USA* (1980)?

11 Tim Robbins played a Vietnam veteran suffering from terrifying hallucinations in what 1990 movie?

12 Name the cold war thriller from 1968, based on an Alistair MacLean novel, with Rock Hudson, Patrick McGoohan and Ernest Borgnine.

13 Who played the lead in the loose biopic on Jimmy Hoffa, the American Trade Union leader in the movie *Hoffa* (1992)?

14 A boy sees his father getting murdered in an alley and grows up with a mission of revenge. Name this 1961 Sam Fuller movie.

15 John Hurt, Tim Roth and Terence Stamp starred in what stylish thriller from 1984?

'I have a face that would stop a sundial.'
– *Charles Laughton*

Answers

1   Jeremy Irons

2   *Lost Highway*

3   Rod Steiger

4   *Airport*, starring Burt Lancaster, Dean Martin, Jacqueline Bisset
     and George Kennedy

5   *The Silence of the Lambs*, directed by Jonathan Demme. It also
     starred Scott Glenn and Chris Isaak

6   *I Walk Alone*

7   *The Firm*. The movie also starred Gene Hackman

8   James Coburn, Sophia Loren and guest star Victor Mature

9   *The Asphalt Jungle*

10   Burt Lancaster and Susan Sarandon

11   *Jacob's Ladder*

12   *Ice Station Zebra*

13   Jack Nicholson. The movie was directed by Danny De Vito

14   *Underworld USA*

15   *The Hit*, directed by Stephen Frears

'Charles Laughton floating in his pool is the reverse of an iceberg,
90% of him is visible.'
– Peter Ustinov

Take 5

1   Can you name the disturbing British thriller from 1970 starring James Fox and Mick Jagger?

2   Name the 1992 British spy drama starring Sam Neill and James Fox.

3   Name the 1960 film in which Russian anarchists barricade themselves in a street in the East End of London.

4   Stanley Kubrick's 1956 thriller starred Sterling Hayden. Name it.

5   Name the swinging sixties thriller starring Michael Caine, Noel Coward and Benny Hill from 1969.

6   What was the 1973 spy thriller directed by Michael Winner featuring Burt Lancaster, Alain Delon and Paul Scofield?

7   Alan Bates was the custodian of various Aboriginal curses, in this 1978 film based on a story by Robert Graves. Name the movie

8   Paul Newman played a private eye in this thriller from 1968. Name the movie.

9   Frank Sinatra starred as a hitman in what cold war spy drama from 1967?

10 Richard Widmark and Henry Fonda starred in what crime thriller from 1968?

11 Who played Agatha Christie's Belgian detective Hercule Poirot in *Murder on the Orient Express* (1974)?

12 Ronald Reagan made his last screen appearance alongside Lee Marvin, Angie Dickinson and John Cassavettes in what 1964 thriller?

13 A shadowy group of businessmen and military leaders plot to assassinate Kennedy. Name this rarely-seen thriller from 1973.

14 Set in the 1930s, can you name this 2002 gangster movie starring Tom Hanks and Paul Newman?

15 Set in the Alaskan midnight sun, what 2002 thriller featured Al Pacino and Robin Williams?

Answers

1   *Performance*, directed by Nicolas Roeg

2   *Hostage*

3   *The Siege of Sidney Street*, starring Donald Sinden, Peter Wyngarde and Kieron Moore

4   *The Killing*

5   *The Italian Job*

6   *Scorpio*

7   *The Shout.* The movie also starred John Hurt and Susannah York

8   *The Moving Target*, also known as *Harper*

9   *The Naked Runner*

10   *Madigan*, directed by Don Siegel

11   Albert Finney. The movie was directed by Sidney Lumet

12   *The Killers*

13   *Executive Action*, starring Burt Lancaster, Robert Ryan and Will Geer

14   *Road to Perdition*, directed by Sam Mendes

15   *Insomnia*

'James Cagney had a quality of authenticity. Bogart was a big fraud.'
– Pat O'Brien

Take 6

1   One of Rock Hudson's finest performances was in this 1966 movie about an elderly businessman getting a chance to live a new existence. Name the movie.

2   Can you name any of the lead players in *The Day They Robbed the Bank of England* (1960)?

3   Who starred as the General and Joint Chief of Staffs in John Frankenheimer's *Seven Days in May* (1963)?

4   This erotic thriller starred William Hurt as a small-town lawyer who falls for femme fatale Kathleen Turner. Name the 1981 movie.

5   'They're young, they're in love and they kill people.' This was the slogan for what stylish, violent crime drama from 1981?

6   Can you name the Bond movie from 1963 with Sean Connery and Robert Shaw?

7   In *The Godfather Part II* (1974) who played the young Don Vito Corleone?

8   Johnny Depp played an FBI undercover agent in a 1997 movie that was set in the 1970s. Can you name it?

9   This movie from 1976 was enough to put you off going to the dentist, as Laurence Olivier worked on Dustin Hoffman's bite to extract information about diamonds. Name the movie.

10   Matt Dillon played a psychopath in what movie from 1991?

11   It was a low-budget tough thriller with Jeffery Hunter and David Janssen. Can you name this 1961 movie?

12   *The Gun Runners* (1958) was based on the Ernest Hemingway novel *To Have and Have Not*. Can you name the two leading stars?

13   Gregory Peck won an Oscar for his performance in what classic crime drama of 1962, based on a Harper Lee novel.

14   Anthony Hopkins starred as an anthropologist who became a killer in what 1999 psychological thriller?

15   Who starred in the remake of *Dial M for Murder* (1954), called *A Perfect Murder* (1998)?

Answers

1   *Seconds*, directed by John Frankenheimer

2   Aldo Ray, Elizabeth Sellars, Peter O'Toole and Kieron Moore

3   Burt Lancaster. The movie also starred Kirk Douglas

4   *Body Heat*

5   *Bonnie and Clyde,* starring Warren Beatty, Faye Dunaway and Gene Hackman. The movie was directed by Arthur Penn

6   *From Russia with Love*, directed by Terence Young. This Ian Fleming book became an even bigger seller when JFK listed it as one of his ten favourite books at the time

7   Robert De Niro. The movie was directed by Francis Ford Coppola

8   *Donnie Brasco*. The movie also starred Mike Newell

9   *Marathon Man*, directed by John Schlesinger

10   *A Kiss Before Dying*

11   *Man-Trap*, directed by actor Edmond O'Brien

12   Audie Murphy and Eddie Albert

13   *To Kill a Mockingbird*

14   *Instinct*. The movie also starred Donald Sutherland

15   Michael Douglas, Gwyneth Paltrow and Viggo Mortensen

'Richard Burton was the Frank Sinatra of Shakespeare.'
– Elizabeth Taylor

SCI-FI
& FANTASY

Take 1

1   Who starred in *The Thing* (1982)?

2   Based on Richard Matheson's novel *I am Legend*, who starred in *The Omega Man* (1971)?

3   Sean Connery starred in what 1979 disaster movie?

4   Leftover robot bits were made into a sculpture that turned into a killer robot. Name this 1980 movie, directed by Richard Stanley.

5   Name the trio of stars in *Demolition Man* (1993).

6   Who played the lead in *TimeCop* (1994)?

7   Who directed *Batman* (1989) and *Batman Returns* (1992)?

8   When was the first *Alien* movie made: 1977, 1979 or 1981?

9   Who starred in *Escape From New York* (1981)?

10 James Woods starred in what 1982 movie directed by David Cronenberg?

11 David Bowie was the alien, Nicolas Roeg was the director. Name this disturbing 1976 movie.

12 Who played the leather-clad avenger Mad Max in the 1979 movie of the same name?

13 Name the on-board computer in Stanley Kubrick's *2001: A Space Odyssey* (1968).

14 Robert Vaughn and Christopher Lee starred in what 1977 science fiction movie?

15 What movie was director John Carpenter's impressive debut in 1974?

'Gossip is the new pornography.'
– *Woody Allen*

nswers

1 Kurt Russell. The movie was directed by John Carpenter

2 Charlton Heston. The movie was directed by Boris Segal

3 *Meteor*. The movie also starred Natalie Wood and Karl Malden

4 *Hardware*, starring Dylan McDermott

5 Sylvester Stallone, Wesley Snipes and Sandra Bullock

6 Jean-Claude Van Damme

7 Tim Burton

8 1979. The movie was directed by Ridley Scott

9 Kurt Russell. The movie was directed by John Carpenter

10 *Videodrome*

11 *The Man Who Fell to Earth*

12 Mel Gibson. The movie was directed by George Miller

13 H.A.L.

14 *Starship Invasions*, directed by Ed Hunt

15 *Dark Star*, made for just $60,000

'A legend in his own lifetime and in his own mind.'
– *Jennifer Lopez (on Jack Nicholson)*

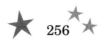

Take 2

1   The classic *2001: A Space Odyssey* (1968) is based on a short story by which sci-fi author?

2   Who was Captain Nemo in *Captain Nemo and the Underwater City* (1969)?

3   Name John Antrobus and Spike Milligan's surreal farce of 1969, set after World War III and starring Ralph Richardson, Michael Hordern, Rita Tushingham, Arthur Lowe and Spike Milligan.

4   Complete the title of Michael Crichton's novel-turned-movie of 1970: *The _____ Strain.*

5   Name the 2003 time travel movie directed by Richard Donner.

6   Directed by Cornel Wilde, name the 1970 movie about a family trying to survive in a world where a created virus is destroying the Earth's crops.

7   Who wrote the novel *A Clockwork Orange* which was made into a movie in 1970?

8   Known for his B-movie horrors, William Castle turned to the topic of flesh-eating insects in what 1975 science fiction movie starring Brad Dillman?

9   Who played the villain Doctor Octopus in *Spider-Man 2* (2004)?

10 An alien planetary federation disapproving of the Earth's atom bomb testing sends down an emissary to warn mankind. Name this 1950s classic movie.

11 How many of the stars can you name in the 1961 version of *The Mysterious Island*, based on Jules Verne's *L'ile Mysterieuse*.

12 Name *The Three Stooges* space outing comedy from 1961.

13 Who provided the voice of the robotic alien spacecraft in *Flight of the Navigator* (1986)?

14 Name the John Carpenter science fiction thriller from 1988 about a hobo who gets involved with a revolutionary movement, whose members use sunglasses to see their enemies.

15 Christopher Plummer and David Warner starred in what 1991 *Star Trek* movie?

Answers

1 Arthur C. Clarke, who co-wrote the screenplay with Stanley Kubrick

2 Robert Ryan. The movie was directed by James Hill

3 *The Bed Sitting Room*, directed by Richard Lester

4 *The Andromeda Strain*, directed by Robert Wise

5 *Timeline*, from a novel by Michael Crichton

6 *No Blade of Grass*. The movie starred Nigel Davenport and Jean Wallace

7 Anthony Burgess, who also wrote the screenplay with director Stanley Kubrick. The film starred Malcolm McDowell and Patrick Magee

8 *Bug*

9 Alfred Molina

10 *The Day the Earth Stood Still*, directed by Robert Wise and starring Michael Rennie

11 Michael Craig, Joan Greenwood, Michael Callan, Gary Merrill and Herbert Lom

12 *The Three Stooges in Orbit*

13 Pee Wee Herman aka Paul Reubens

14 *They Live*

15 *Star Trek VI: The Undiscovered Country*. Directed by Nicholas Meyer, the movie starred William Shatner and Leonard Nimoy

'An actor who I won't name says that whenever an interviewer asks him what has been a low point in his life, he likes to answer, "this interview".'
– Peter Finch

Take 3

1 This 1936 sci-fi movie was Boris Karloff's first appearance as a mad scientist. The film also starred Bela Lugosi. Can you name it?

2 Who played He-Man in *Masters of the Universe* (1987)?

3 Arnie Schwarzenegger was a commando leader on a covert mission in Central American jungles being stalked by an alien who killed humans for sport. Name this 1987 movie.

4 Paul Verhoeven directed what popular 1987 movie starring Peter Weller as a very unusual policeman?

5 Mark Hamill, Bob Peck and Bill Paxton starred in what British science fiction film from 1989?

6 Name the 1989 move in which a desert community was terrorised by man-eating, sand-burrowing worms.

7 Ray Milland directed and starred in what 1962 science fiction movie about people trying to survive after a nuclear blast in Los Angeles?

8 What black singer turned actor starred in *The World, The Flesh, and The Devil* (1959)?

9 Who starred in *Journey to the Centre of the Earth* (1959) based on Jules Verne's novel?

10 Sam Neill and Lawrence Fishburne starred in what 1997 science fiction film set on the far side of the universe?

11 Name the two stars of the box-office flop *Supernova* (2000)?

12 Who directed *Superman II (1980)* and *Superman III* (1983)?

13 Who played the male leads in *Armageddon* (1998), directed by Michael Bay?

14 Roland Emmerich directed Kurt Russell and James Spader in what 1994 science fiction film?

15 What was the name of David Cronenberg's 'exploding-head' movie from 1981?

Answers

1   *The Invisible Ray*

2   Dolph Lundgren. The movie also starred Frank Langella

3   *Predator*

4   *Robocop*

5   *Slipstream*

6   *Tremors*. The movie starred Kevin Bacon

7   *Panic in Year Zero*

8   Harry Belafonte. The movie also starred Inger Stevens

9   Pat Boone and James Mason

10 *Event Horizon*

11 James Spader and Angela Bassett

12 Richard Lester

13 Bruce Willis, Ben Affleck and Billy Bob Thornton

14 *Stargate*

15 *Scanners*

'You make a hit the same way you make a flop.'
– *Robert De Niro*

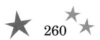

Take 4

1   David Lynch directed what 1984 big screen epic, based on the novel by Frank Herbert?

2   Based on Whitley Strieber's book about alien abduction, in what 1990 film did Christopher Walken star as the author?

3   Name the classic 1953 science fiction movie about invaders from Mars, based on a novel by H.G. Wells.

4   Jane Fonda and Michael Douglas starred in what 1979 movie about a faulty nuclear reactor?

5   Name the 1971 movie starring Bruce Dern in which he was cut adrift with his very own 'Garden of Eden'.

6   Arnold Schwarzenegger played a man suffering from nightmares about Mars, a place he'd never been to. Name this action-packed movie from 1990.

7   Who played the Joker in *Batman* (1989)?

8   *Slaughterhouse-Five* (1972) was director George Roy Hill's film version of a famous science fiction book. Who wrote the novel?

9   Name director Luc Besson's clever and witty 1997 film, set in the twenty-third century.

10   Who starred in *Tron* (1982)?

11   Val Kilmer, Tom Sizemore, Carrie-Ann Moss and Terence Stamp starred in what film from 2000 which was a mix of sci-fi and horror?

12   Sean Connery starred in a 1974 sci-fi movie directed by John Boorman. What was it called?

13   The British science fiction classic *Village of the Damned* (1960), starring George Sanders, is based on which book?

14   Name the 1957 black and white science fiction classic, directed by Jack Arnold and starring Grant Williams, regarded as one of the finest of the genre.

15   Who played the rather nasty Dr Smith in the 1997 big budget version of the 1960s TV series *Lost in Space*?

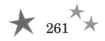

Answers

1   *Dune*, starring Francesca Annis, Kyle MacLachlan, Sting and Max Von Sydow

2   *Communion*

3   *The War of the Worlds*

4   *The China Syndrome*. The movie also starred Jack Lemmon and Scott Brady

5   *Silent Running*

6   *Total Recall*. Directed by Paul Verhoeven, the movie also starred Sharon Stone

7   Jack Nicholson. Michael Keaton was Batman and Tim Burton directed.

8   Kurt Vonnegut Junior

9   *The Fifth Element*, starring Bruce Willis, Milla Jovovich, Ian Holm Gary Oldman and Chris Tucker

10 Jeff Bridges

11 *Red Planet*

12 *Zardoz*

13 *The Midwich Cuckoos* by John Wyndham

14 *The Incredible Shrinking Man*

15 Gary Oldman. The movie was directed by Stephen Hopkins

'Long ago Hollywood decided that the way to keep people quiet is to overpay them.'
– William Goldman

Take 5

Lord of the Rings – FELLOWSHIP OF THE RING (2001)

1 Name the nine companions who formed the Fellowship of the Ring?

2 At Bilbo's birthday party he announced his age. How old was he?

3 Name the Inn where Frodo met Aragorn for the first time.

4 What did the Hobbits call the land where they lived?

5 As Frodo and Sam were about to leave The Shire they encountered Merry and Pippin stealing food from a farm. Who owned the farm?

6 What happened to Frodo's Elvish sword when Orcs were nearby?

7 How did Gimli attempt to destroy the Ring?

8 What role did English actor Andy Serkis play in the trilogy?

9 In Rivendell Bilbo gave Frodo a gift which later saved his life. What was it?

10 Where did the Fellowship encounter a creature called the Balrog?

11 What does Gandalf say to his companions just before he falls to his doom: 'Fly, you Fools', 'Run, you fools', or 'Go, you fools'?

12 Which world famous singer was said to be interested in playing Elrond, having previously appeared in a movie as Jareth, King of the Goblins?

13 Which actor, in real life, was the tallest member of the Fellowship?

14 Which actor in the movie was the only member of the cast to have actually met J.R.R. Tolkien?

15 Which character said the words that make up the subtitle of the film?

'I'm the only director who ever made two pictures with Marilyn Monroe.
Forget the Oscar, I deserve the Purple Heart.'
– Billy Wilder

Answers

1. Frodo, Sam, Merry, Pippin, Gandalf, Aragorn, Legolas, Gimli and Boromir

2. 111 years old

3. The Prancing Pony

4. The Shire

5. Farmer Maggot

6. It glowed blue

7. He tried to smash it with his axe

8. Gollum

9. A vest made of Elvish metal

10. The mines of Moria

11. 'Fly, you Fools'

12. David Bowie

13. John Rhys-Davies, playing Gimli the dwarf!

14. Christopher Lee

15. Elrond, Lord of Rivendell, described the troop of nine as 'The Fellowship of the Ring'

'It's not the men in your life that counts. It's the life in your men.'
– *Mae West*

Take 6

Lord of the Rings – THE TWO TOWERS (2002)

1 Miranda Otto played the part of Éowyn of Rohan, but which Irish actress was first offered the part?

2 John Rhys-Davies played two characters in this movie. Who were they?

3 Viggo Mortensen was injured by a steel helmet in filming. How?

4 What animal was used to produce the sound of the fell beasts ridden by the Ringwraiths?

5 When Frodo and Sam were brought as prisoners to Osgiliath by Faramir, Sam said: 'By rights we shouldn't even be here'. Why was this statement true?

6 What happened to the horse ridden by Aragorn after the shoot?

7 What did actor Andy Serkis claim was the inspiration for Gollum's voice?

8 What was unusual about some of the Rohirrim, the riders of Rohan?

9 Bernard Hill played the part of King Theoden, but was originally considered for which role?

10 Which character said the words that make up the subtitle of the film?

11 How long did it take to build the set at Helm's Deep: 7 weeks, 3 months or 7 months?

12 How did Peter Jackson create the sound of the Orc army for the battle at Helm's Deep?

13 Who was Grima Wormtongue referring to when he said: 'Stormcrow'?

14 What was Peter Jackson's cameo appearance in *The Two Towers*?

15 What happened to the Orc who followed Merry and Pippin into Fangorn Forest?

Answers

1 Alison Doody, who had to turn it down because of family commitments

2 Gimli, and he was also the voice of Treebeard

3 When Aragorn, Gimli and Legolas were in pursuit of the captured Merry and Pippin they came across a burning mound of slain Orcs. A steel helmet on the ground was kicked in rage by Aragorn causing Viggo Mortensen to break two toes

4 A donkey

5 In Tolkien's book Frodo and Sam are not taken by Faramir to Osgiliath

6 Viggo Mortensen became so fond of the horse that he bought it from the owners

7 The sound of a cat coughing up a fur-ball

8 Many of them were actually women wearing false beards

9 Gandalf

10 Saruman, in a voice-over, as the towers of Isengard and Mordor are shown on screen

11 7 months

12 Jackson himself led thousands of cricket fans in a stadium as they screamed out the required battle cries, written on the stadium's giant screen

13 Gandalf

14 A chain-mailed defender of Helm's Deep

15 He was stepped on and squashed by Treebeard

'There is nothing the British like better than a bloke who comes from nowhere, makes it, and then gets clobbered.'
– *Melvyn Bragg*

Take 7

Lord of the Rings – RETURN OF THE KING (2003)

1 Which character says the words that make up the film's subtitle?

2 What connection did actor Sean Astin have with his character Samwise Gamgee's daughter Elanor?

3 Who came up with the idea of King Theoden touching the spears of his front-line men with his sword just before they charge into battle?

4 What was the connection between this movie and J.R.R. Tolkien's great grandson Royd Tolkien?

5 The last words in the movie were also the last words in Tolkien's book. What were they and who said them?

6 How many Oscars did *Return of the King* win?

7 The *Lord of the Rings* Trilogy received the most Academy Award Nominations of any film series. How many nominations: 21, 28, 30?

8 *Return of the King* became only the second film to pass one billion dollars in sales. Which film was the first to do this?

9 How did Gollum deceive Frodo and turn him against Sam?

10 Peter Jackson made yet another cameo appearance, as what?

11 Who composed, orchestrated and conducted the music for *The Lord of the Rings*?

12 Which British singer, famous for her hits with musician Dave Stewart, sang 'Into the West' on the soundtrack?

13 What did Peter Jackson give to Orlando Bloom as a souvenir of his role as Legolas?

14 The *Lord of the Rings* trilogy was filmed simultaneously. What was the total production time span: 3 years, 5 years or 7 years?

15 The giant arachnid Shelob is based on what kind of spider found in New Zealand?

Answers

1   Gandalf – in the scene with Denethor, Steward of Gondor, where he tells him he can't refuse 'the return of the king'

2   Elanor was played by Sean's real-life daughter Alexandra

3   Bernard Hill (King Theoden)

4   Royd Tolkien appeared in a cameo role as a Ranger of Gondor

5   'Well I'm back', spoken by Samwise Gamgee

6   Eleven Oscars

7   30 nominations. (The *Star Wars* series got 21 and *The Godfather* trilogy got 28)

8   *Titanic* (1997)

9   He convinced him that Sam had stolen and eaten the last of the lembas bread and was getting ready to take the ring

10   He was a mercenary on a boat

11   Howard Shore

12   Annie Lennox

13   His bow

14   7 years

15   The tunnel web spider

Take 8

Star Wars

1   Which well-known American actor provided the voice for Darth Vader?

2   Which robot was the tallest: R2D2 or C3PO?

3   Which character was played by Harrison Ford?

4   How many years separated the making of *Star Wars* (1977) and *Star Wars Episode I: The Phantom Menace*: 19, 21 or 22?

5   Which *Muppet* character featured in the 1980 sequel *The Empire Strikes Back*?

6   What was Liam Neeson's character called in *The Phantom Menace* (1999)?

7   What was the name of the large moon-shaped space vessel in *Star Wars* (1977)?

8   What was Han Solo's spaceship called?

9   What was Darth Vader's original name?

10   Who played the part of the young Obi-Wan Kenobi in *The Phantom Menace* (1999)?

11   What was the traditional weapon of a Jedi Knight?

12   Carrie Fisher (Princess Leia) has famous parents. Who are they?

13   George Lucas set up a special effects company for *Star Wars*, which has been busily involved in films ever since. What is it called?

14   How many films, in total, did George Lucas suggest would make up the full *Star Wars* series?

15   Mel Brooks filmed a parody of *Star Wars* starring John Candy, Rick Moranis and the director himself. Name the 1987 movie.

'Take away the pop eyes, the cigarette and those funny clipped words and what have you got?'
– Joan Crawford (on Bette Davis)

Answers

1   James Earl Jones

2   C3PO

3   Han Solo

4   22 years

5   Yoda (Frank Oz)

6   Qui-Gon Jinn

7   The Death Star

8   The Millennium Falcon

9   Anakin Skywalker

10   Ewan McGregor

11   The light-sabre

12   Singer Eddie Fisher and actress Debbie Reynolds

13   Industrial Light and Magic

14   Nine

15   *Spaceballs*

'*Schindler's List* . . . is an exploitation film.'
– *David Mamet*

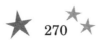

SHAKESPEARE

Take 1

1   Who directed and starred in *Richard III* (1955)?

2   Who played Clarence in the above movie?

3   It was a comedy from 1942 starring Jack Benny. Name the movie. (Clue: It's a line from *Hamlet*)

4   Who directed *The Great Garrick* (1937) starring Brian Aherne as David Garrick?

5   Who starred as the lovestruck leads in *Romeo and Juliet* (1936)?

6   Who played Tybalt and Mercutio in the above movie?

7   In the 1954 version of *Romeo and Juliet*, who played Romeo?

8   In *A Midsummer Night's Dream* (1935) who played Bottom and Puck?

9   The movie *Ran* (1985) was inspired by what Shakespearean play?

10 Who directed *Ran* (1985)?

11 Movie critic Leonard Maltin called it a pretentious mess! Released in 1987, it was a spoof on King Lear and starred Peter Sellers, Woody Allen and Burgess Meredith. Can you name the director and the movie?

12 Who played Ophelia in Laurence Olivier's movie *Hamlet* (1948)?

13 Who played Hamlet in a 1962 German movie version of the play?

14 In what John Ford movie of 1946 does Victor Mature quote some of Hamlet's lines?

15 Who said 'If Shakespeare were alive now, he'd be writing for the cinema'?

'She speaks five languages and can't act in any of them.'
– *John Gielgud (on Ingrid Bergman)*

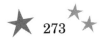

Answers

1   Laurence Olivier

2   John Gielgud

3   *To Be Or Not To Be*

4   James Whale, famous for *Frankenstein* (1931), starring Boris Karloff

5   Leslie Howard and Norma Shearer

6   Basil Rathbone was Tybalt, and John Barrymore played Mercutio

7   Laurence Harvey

8   James Cagney was Bottom, and Mickey Rooney played Puck

9   *King Lear*

10 Akira Kurosawa

11 Jean-Luc Godard was the director and the movie was called *King Lear: Fear and Loathing*

12 Jean Simmons. Laurence Olivier played Hamlet

13 Maximilian Schell

14 *My Darling Clementine*

15 Al Pacino

'There used to be a me, but I had it surgically removed.'
– Peter Sellers

Take 2

1 In what country was Laurence Olivier's film version of *Henry V* (1944) shot?

2 Who wrote the music score for the above movie?

3 Name the three leads in *A Midsummer Night's Dream* (1999)

4 What Shakespeare play did Kenneth Branagh adapt for his 1993 movie, in which he starred alongside his then wife Emma Thompson?

5 What happened to Orson Welles' planned movie *The Merchant of Venice* (1969)?

6 Who directed the young Olivia Hussey and Leonard Whiting in *Romeo and Juliet* (1968)?

7 Which Irish actor played Friar Laurence in the above movie?

8 Who played Macbeth in the 1948 USA movie of the same name?

9 Which famous married couple of the time starred in *The Taming of the Shrew* (1966), directed by Franco Zeffirelli?

10 In the 1995 film version of *Richard III*, who played Richard III?

11 What were Richard III's last words in the play?

12 Name the famous horror stars who appeared in the movie *The Tower of London* (1939).

13 What was the name of the American musical of 1953 based on *The Taming of the Shrew*, starring Howard Keel and Kathryn Grayson?

14 Which famous English actor was the narrator in *Romeo and Juliet* (1968)?

15 Who starred in the GB production of *A Winter's Tale* (1966)?

'I'd rather watch old Doris Day movies than the Oscars.'
– Orson Welles

Answers

1   Ireland

2   William Walton

3   Kevin Kline, Michelle Pfeiffer and Rupert Everett

4   *Much Ado About Nothing*

5   Two reels of the film and the soundtrack were stolen from the production office in Rome

6   Franco Zeffirelli

7   Milo O'Shea

8   Orson Welles

9   Richard Burton and Elizabeth Taylor

10 Ian McKellen

11 'A horse! A horse! My kingdom for a horse!'

12 Basil Rathbone was Richard III, Boris Karloff played Mord, and Vincent Price was Clarence

13 *Kiss Me Kate*

14 Laurence Olivier

15 Laurence Harvey and Jane Asher

'I may not be as good as Laurence Olivier but I'm taller.'
– *Roger Moore*

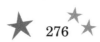

Take 3

1   In *Hamlet, Scène de Duel* (France 1900) what famous actress of the era played Hamlet?

2   What horror duo had cameo roles in *Hamlet* (1948)?

3   Who was the voice of the ghost in the above movie?

4   In the remake of *Henry V* (1989) who played Henry V and directed the movie?

5   Who played the French king in the above movie?

6   In Peter Greenaway's *Prospero's Books* (1991) who played Prospero?

7   In the comedy movie *The Magic Christian* (1969) starring Peter Sellers and Ringo Starr, who does a striptease while performing *Hamlet*?

8   Who played the gravedigger in *Hamlet* (1949)?

9   In the 1996 version of *Hamlet*, who played Ophelia?

10 Who directed *King Lear* (1970), starring Paul Scofield as King Lear?

11 Which Irish actor played the fool in the above movie?

12 Which Irish actor played Macduff in *Macbeth* (1948)?

13 In the 1993 version of *Much Ado About Nothing* who starred in the parts of Beatrice and Don Pedro?

14 In *Othello* (1951), who played Othello and Iago?

15 Who portrayed Othello and Iago in the 1995 version of the movie *Othello*?

'My marriage license reads, to whom it may concern.'
– Mickey Rooney (married 8 times)

Answers

1   Sarah Bernhardt

2   Peter Cushing and Christopher Lee

3   John Gielgud

4   Kenneth Branagh

5   Paul Scofield

6   John Gielgud

7   Laurence Harvey

8   Stanley Holloway

9   Kate Winslet

10   Sir Peter Brook

11   Jack MacGowran

12   Dan O'Herlihy

13   Emma Thompson and Denzel Washington

14   Orson Welles and Micheál MacLiammóir

15   Laurence Fishburne and Kenneth Branagh

'There's something sexy about a gut. Not a 400-pound beer gut,
but a little paunch. I love that.'
– *Sandra Bullock*

Take 4

1   In *Shakespeare in Love* (1998) who played Will Shakespeare?

2   What hugely successful Disney animation movie from 1994 adapted the storyline from Shakespeare's *Hamlet*?

3   In *Hamlet* (1990) Mel Gibson played Hamlet, but who played his mother, Gertrude?

4   Who directed the above movie?

5   What was Laurence Olivier's first Shakespearean screen role?

6   What happened to Mickey Rooney during the 1935 movie production of *A Midsummer Night's Dream*?

7   What Laurel and Hardy movie from 1936 was loosely based on Shakespeare's *A Comedy Of Errors*?

8   In Derek Jarman's *The Tempest* (1979) who played Prospero?

9   Can you name the 1957 movie, which was a loose adaptation of *Macbeth* from director Akira Kurosawa?

10   Name the romantic drama from 1965 about strolling players.

11   In *Theatre of Blood* (GB 1973) who played the supposedly dead Shakespearean actor who planned to murder his drama critics.

12   In what 1974 movie did Spike Milligan and Peter Sellers star, and get a chance to perform *Macbeth*?

13   In *The Dressser* (1983) who played the great Shakespearean actor who was losing it?

14   In what 1993 movie was Arnold Schwarzenegger seen briefly playing *Hamlet*?

15   In what 1989 movie did Robin Williams mimic John Wayne quoting Shakespeare?

'The first time I met Steven Spielberg he gave me the script for *American Beauty*.
The last two times he has given me awards.'
– Sam Mendes

Answers

1 Joseph Fiennes

2 *The Lion King*

3 Glenn Close

4 Franco Zeffirelli

5 He played Orlando in *As You Like It* (1936)

6 He broke his leg and had to be moved around the set on a bicycle!

7 *Our Relations*

8 Heathcote Williams

9 *Throne of Blood*

10 *Shakespeare Wallah*

11 Vincent Price

12 *The Great McGonagall*

13 Albert Finney (with more than a hint of Donald Wolfit). It also starred Tom Courtenay as his dresser

14 *Last Action Hero*

15 *Dead Poets Society*

'I'm just a hair away from being a serial killer.'
– Dennis Hopper

Take 5

1   What is the opening line of *Twelfth Night*?

2   In the 1953 movie *Julius Caesar* who played Marc Antony?

3   Name the 1955 gangster movie, starring Paul Douglas, loosely based on *Macbeth*.

4   Who directed the Playboy Productions of *Macbeth* (1971), starring Jon Finch?

5   Who directed and starred in *Antony and Cleopatra* (1972)?

6   In the *Prince of Players* (USA 1954) Richard Burton does scenes from *Romeo and Juliet*, *Richard III* and *Hamlet*. What famous actor from the late 19th century was he portraying in this movie?

7   In *The Taming of the Shrew* (USA 1929) who played Petruchio and Katherine?

8   In the 1968 Royal Shakespeare Company's version of *A Midsummer Night's Dream* who played Titania and Oberon?

9   In the 1911 recorded version of the play *Henry VIII*, what famous Shakespearean actor of the time played the title role?

10 In *Chimes at Midnight* (1966) who played Sir John Falstaff?

11 What classic musical from 1961 was based on *Romeo and Juliet*?

12 Who played Titus in the 1999 movie of the same title?

13 What Shakespearean play was turned into a movie in 1995 and starred Ben Kingsley and Nigel Hawthorne?

14 In the movie *Looking for Richard* (1996) who directed and played Richard III?

15 Which famous actor's son played Macbeth in the 1997 UK version?

'I've done an awful lot of stuff that's a monument to public patience.'
– Tyrone Power

Answers

1   'If music be the food of love, play on . . .'

2   Marlon Brando

3   *Joe Macbeth*

4   Roman Polanski

5   Charlton Heston

6   Edwin Booth

7   Douglas Fairbanks Senior and Mary Pickford

8   Judi Dench and Ian Richardson

9   Herbert Beerbohm Tree. He insisted the film be destroyed only months after it was shown

10 Orson Welles, who also directed it

11 *West Side Story*, starring Natalie Wood and Richard Beymer

12 Anthony Hopkins (Titus Andronicus)

13 Twelfth Night

14 Al Pacino

15 Sean Connery's son Jason

'People think I've got an interesting walk. I'm just trying to hold my stomach in.'
– Robert Mitchum

Take 6

1   In what 1957 movie does Charlie Chaplin quote a soliloquy from *Hamlet*?

2   At a birthday party quiz, Ralph Fiennes and Paul Scofield give short quotes from Shakespeare's *Macbeth*, *Measure For Measure*, *Much Ado About Nothing* and *The Merchant Of Venice*. Can you name the 1994 movie?

3   Name the two leads in *Rosencrantz And Guildenstern Are Dead* (1990).

4   In *Hamlet* (1969), starring Nichol Williamson as Hamlet, who played Claudius and Ophelia?

5   Because of bad reviews, Richard Burton ordered the prints to be destroyed of his performance as Hamlet in NY City. Fortunately for us some prints survived. Who directed and starred in the filmed play?

6   What actor suffers from playing Othello in *A Double Life* (1948)?

7   What was so different about Kenneth Branagh's movie *Hamlet* (1996) compared to other film versions?

8   What was the connection between *Doctor Zhivago* (1965) and the Russian version of *King Lear* (1970)?

9   Franco Zeffirelli made a film version of Verdi's opera, *Otello* in 1986. Who played the doomed Moor?

10 Why did Roman Polanski's *Macbeth* (1971) receive such abuse by the film critics at the time of its release?

11 What caused unintentional laughter among the audience while watching *As You Like It* (1936)?

12 What part did Michael York play in *Romeo and Juliet* (1968)?

13 What Shakespearean play did Kenneth Brannagh turn into a romantic musical comedy in 1999?

14 Who refused Laurence Olivier permission to cast his then wife in the 1944 version of *Henry V*?

15 In the 1989 version of *Henry V*, who played Sir John Falstaff?

Answers

1   *A King In New York*, directed by Charlie Chaplin

2   *The Quiz Show*

3   Gary Oldman and Tim Roth. The movie was based on Tom Stoppard's play and directed by him. The characters' names are from Shakespeare's *Hamlet*

4   Anthony Hopkins played Claudius and Marianne Faithfull was Ophelia

5   John Gielgud

6   Ronald Colman

7   Branagh filmed the complete unabridged play (232 minutes)

8   Boris Pasternak wrote Zhivago and did the Russian translation of *King Lear*, which was used in the movie

9   Placido Domingo

10   Because he had Francesca Annis, who played Lady Macbeth, perform naked during her sleepwalking scene

11   Elizabeth Bergner, who played the main character, Rosalind, had a strong German accent and mispronounced several words.

12   He played Tybalt

13   *Love's Labour Lost*

14   David O. Selznick, who thought the part of Katherine in the film was too small for a star

15   Robbie Coltrane

'Politics is for people who are too ugly to get into show business.'
– Bill Clinton

ANIMATION

Take 1

1 Who made *The Wrong Trousers* (1993), a classic Wallace and Gromit stop-motion animation?

2 Regarded as the father of animation, he made *Gertie the Dinosaur* (1914). Can you name him?

3 Which cartoon character had his first starring role in 1941?

4 Who made the powerful *Faust* (1994) using live action, stop-motion animation and puppetry?

5 Name the actor who voiced Rocky in *Chicken Run* (2000)?

6 Although fired from the project, Richard Williams went on to win an Oscar for what hugely successful 1988 live action and animated movie starring Bob Hoskins?

7 Name the cartoon rodent hero, created by Paul Terry, that was a spoof on Superman.

8 Name the two cartoon birds that rose to fame after their first movie, *Talking Magpies* (1946)?

9 Regarded as Bugs Bunny's finest hour where he and Elmer are in a Wagnerian opera, name this 1957 Chuck Jones classic.

10 Hanna and Barbera are regarded as the founders of TV animation with such classics as *Yogi Bear* and *The Jetsons*. What were their first names?

11 Name the cartoon movie from 1955 based on a George Orwell book.

12 Who teamed with the Monty Python crew and did some excellent animation as well as directing some of their hit movies?

13 Complete the name of this legendary director of many a *Looney Tunes* and *Merrie Melodies*: Friz _____.

14 Complete the name of the Warner Brothers cartoon cowboy character _____ *Sam* who was always gunning for Bugs Bunny.

15 What was Sylvester the Cat's catch phrase?

Answers

1. Nick Park

2. Windsor McKay

3. Woody Woodpecker, whose voice was provided by Grace Stafford

4. Jan Svankmajer. Born in Prague in 1934, he also enjoys a 'cult' following as a moviemaker

5. Mel Gibson. The movie was directed by Nick Park and Peter Lord

6. *Who Framed Roger Rabbit?*

7. *Mighty Mouse*. He was called Super Mouse in his first four movie cartoons

8. Heckle and Jeckle

9. *What's Opera Doc?* (1957)

10. William Hanna and Joseph Barbera

11. *Animal Farm*, a Halas and Batchelor creation

12. Terry Gilliam

13. Friz Freleng

14. *Yosemite Sam*

15. 'Sufferin' Succotash!'

'If you ask me if I'm the luckiest guy in the world, all I can say is "Yup".'
– Gary Cooper

Take 2

1   Beginning in 1933, name the popular series about a sailor and his girlfriend.

2   What creative team made the animated version of *Gulliver's Travels* (1939)?

3   Who was the first sex symbol cartoon star and what was her catch phrase?

4   What animated film from 1972 was the first to receive an 'x' rating?

5   Who is the most famous cartoon rabbit in the world?

6   Who made his first screen debut in *Porky Duck Hunt* (1937)?

7   What is Porky's catch phrase?

8   Name the rooster in many of Warner Brothers cartoon shorts.

9   Who was the fastest mouse in Mexico?

10 Did Wile E. Coyote ever catch the road runner in a movie?

11 What was Tweety Bird's catch phrase whenever Sylvester the Cat's plans backfired?

12 Who was once dubbed 'the man of a thousand voices'.

13 What 1994 live action/animated film featured the talents of Macaulay Culkin, Whoopi Goldberg and Leonard Nimoy?

14 Who were the non-cartoon stars who worked with Bugs Bunny and Daffy Duck in *Looney Tunes: Back in Action* (2004)?

15 Who was the voice of Hazel in *Watership Down* (1978)?

'My dad used to tell me, "You know, you got to get a haircut," and I'd say,
"What is the matter with that old man? Doesn't he know how cool I look?"
But looking back at the prom pictures, I feel bad for every girl.'
– *Adam Sandler*

Answers

1   *Popeye*

2   The Fleischer Brothers

3   Betty Boop. Her catchphrase was 'Boop-Boop-A-Doop'

4   *Fritz the Cat*

5   Bugs Bunny

6   Daffy Duck

7   'B-b-b-big deal!'

8   Foghorn Leghorn

9   Speedy Gonzales

10   Yes, once in *Soup or Sonic*

11   'Bad ol' putty tat!'

12   Mel Blanc. who gave voice to Bugs Bunny, Daffy Duck, Tweety Bird, Sylvester the Cat, Porky Pig and many more

13   *The Pagemaster*

14   Brendan Fraser, Jenna Elfman and Steve Martin

15   John Hurt

Grace Stafford voiced the popular Woody Woodpecker,
which was created by her husband, Walter Lanz.

Take 3

1   In what classic Disney movie from 1940 was Mickey Mouse an apprentice to a sorcerer?

2   In *Dumbo* (1941) what was the name of the mouse that befriended Dumbo?

3   Name the boisterous baby rabbit in *Bambi* (1942).

4   Complete the title of this Disney animation from 1941: *The _____ Dragon*.

5   Who gave the voice to Ichabod Crane in *The Legend of Sleepy Hollow* (1949), based on Washington Irving's nineteenth century tale?

6   What was the name of the old panther in *The Jungle Book* (1967), a film loosely based on Rudyard Kipling's book?

7   Who did the voice of the Mad Hatter in *Alice in Wonderland* (1951)?

8   What was the name of Peter Pan's fairy companion in the movie *Peter Pan* (1953), based on J.M. Barrie's writings?

9   Live action and animation featured in what 1946 movie, based on the *Uncle Remus* fables by Joel Chandler Harris?

10 Name the three good fairies in *Sleeping Beauty* (1959)?

11 What were the names of the Banks children in *Mary Poppins* (1964)?

12 Name the 1955 movie about a lovestruck spaniel and a mongrel.

13 Who was Pinocchio's elderly creator in the movie *Pinocchio* (1940)?

14 Disney's classic *Snow White and the Seven Dwarfs* (1937) was inspired by what storytellers?

15 What was the first Mickey Mouse short?

'Let's say I've given up being moody magnificence
but my friends still say I'm mean.'
– *Jane Russell*

Answers

1. *Fantasia*

2. Timothy Mouse

3. Thumper

4. *The Reluctant Dragon*

5. Bing Crosby

6. Bagheera, with the voice of Sebastion Cabot

7. The talented Ed Wynn

8. Tinkerbell

9. *Song of the South*

10. Flora, Fauna and Merryweather. The bad fairy was Maleficent

11. Jane and Michael

12. *Lady and the Tramp*. This hugely successful movie was filmed in Cinemascope

13. Geppetto

14. Jakob and Wilhelm Grimm

15. *Plane Crazy* (1928). *Steam Boat Willie* (1928), the third Mickey Mouse short, was generally credited as the first animated movie to have sound

'If you're going through hell, keep going.'
– *Walt Disney*

Take 4

1   What was the name of the orang-utan in *The Jungle Book* (1967)?

2   Name Mickey Mouse's girlfriend.

3   What Disney movie from 1960 featured a most colourful villain called Cruella DeVil.

4   Name the 1963 movie about a young King Arthur.

5   In Disney's *Robin Hood* (1973), what were Robin and Marian?

6   Complete the title of this Disney movie from 1969: *It's* ____ ____ ____ *Bird*.

7   Who were the voices of the mice in *The Rescuers* (1977)?

8   Name the lion that Jeremy Irons gave voice to in *The Lion King* (1994)?

9   What 1991 movie featured the song 'A Whole New World'?

10 It was a retelling of the classic fable about a young woman who had to live with a hideous creature. Name this 1991 animated movie.

11 Name the 1989 Disney movie that was based on the fairy tale by Hans Christian Anderson.

12 Who did the voice for Professor Ratigan in *Basil, The Great Mouse Detective* (1986)?

13 Complete the title of Disney's 1985 movie: *The Black* _____.

14 Name the 1990 movie in which mice duo Bernard and Bianca come to the help of a young boy.

15 Who voiced the Genie in *Aladdin* (1992)?

'If you really want to torture me, sit me in a room strapped down to a chair and put Mariah Carey on over and over again. That would be eternal hell for me. I mean it. The worst.'
– *Cameron Diaz*

Answers

1   King Louie

2   Minnie Mouse

3   *101 Dalmatians*

4   *The Sword and the Stone*, based loosely on T.H. White's *The Once and Future King*

5   Foxes

6   *It's Tough Being a Bird*, which won an Academy Award

7   Bob Newman (Bernard) and Eva Gabor (Miss Bianca)

8   Scar

9   *Aladdin.* The movie won an Academy Award for Best Original Score and Song

10   *Beauty and the Beast*

11   *The Little Mermaid*

12   Vincent Price

13   *The Black Cauldron*

14   *The Rescuers Down Under*

15   Robin Williams

'Speeches from Oscar winners should be limited to one minute,
during which they are required by law to thank their cosmetic surgeon and
point out, with visual aids, their most recent nips, tucks and enlargements.'
– Denis Leary

Take 5

1   What Winnie the Pooh movie won an Academy Award in 1968?

2   In what Mickey Mouse movie of 1933 did cartoon versions of Greta Garbo, Laurel and Hardy, Mae West, Joan Crawford, Buster Keaton and other Hollywood luminaries appear?

3   Name Donald Duck's furry adversaries?

4   Name Mickey Mouse's dog.

5   What was Mickey Mouse's first colour movie in 1935?

6   Name the 1995 movie, set in the American wilderness of the 1600s, about a Native American princess growing up.

7   Who sang the songs for Willie the Whale in *The Whale Who Wanted to Sing at the Met* (1946)?

8   What was the name of the Owl in *The Sword and the Stone* (1963)?

9   Name the two Dalmatian lovers in *101 Dalmatians* (1960).

10 What animated movie of 1999, with the voice talents of Glenn Close, Brian Blessed, Minnie Driver and Tony Goldwyn, was based on Edgar Rice Burroughs' creation?

11 Name the 1998 movie about a young Chinese girl who dons male clothing and goes to war to save her family honour.

12 Name the partly animated fantasy feature from 1944 starring Donald Duck and his friends Panchito and Joe Carioca.

13 What is the name of Donald Duck's girlfriend?

14 What feature sea adventure did the Disney team make in 2003?

15 An orphaned kitten ends up in the company of a band of pickpocket dogs. Can you name this 1988 movie?

'I'll never go back to Cannes
– that whole thing is as phony as the Academy Awards.'
– *Mickey Rourke*

Answers

1 *Winnie the Pooh and the Blustery Day*

2 *Mickey's Gala Premiere*

3 The chipmunks Chip and Dale

4 Pluto

5 *The Band Concert*

6 *Pocahontas*

7 Nelson Eddy, who also narrated the movie

8 Archimedes

9 Ponga and Perdita

10 *Tarzan*

11 *Mulan.* The snappy little dragon was given voice by the talented Eddie Murphy

12 *The Three Caballeros*

13 Daisy

14 *Finding Nemo*

15 *Oliver and Company*, inspired by Charles Dickens' *Oliver Twist*

'I have never met anyone as utterly mean as Marilyn Monroe
nor as utterly fabulous on screen.'
– *Billy Wilder*

Take 6

1   What movie won Walt Disney his first Academy Award in 1932?

2   What Silly Symphony cartoon won Disney his second in 1933?

3   Where was Walt Disney born: Chicago, New York or Florida?

4   A mammoth, a sloth and a sabre-tooth tiger formed an unlikely team in what popular 2002 animated film?

5   Name the 'bug' that was called on to be Pinocchio's 'conscience' by the blue fairy?

6   Name Donald Duck's nephews.

7   Mickey Rooney was the voice of Tod, Kurt Russell was Copper and Pearl Bailey was Big Mamma. What was this 1981 movie?

8   Duchess and her three kittens were abandoned in the countryside by the butler and had to make their way home to Paris. Name the 1970 movie.

9   In 1983 Disney studios made a charming movie adapted from a Charles Dickens story. What was the movie?

10 Angela Lansbury, David Tomlinson and Roddy McDowall starred in what 1971 Disney movie?

11 Who was the voice of Thomas O'Malley in *The Aristocats* (1970)?

12 What was the name of the albatross who carried Bernard and Bianca on their journey in *The Rescuers* (1977)?

13 Who was the voice of Scrooge McDuck in *Mickey's Christmas Carol* (1983)?

14 Who played the man whom couldn't stop laughing in *Mary Poppins* (1964)?

15 In what year and in what movie did Disney's Donald Duck first appear?

'Marriage is like the army. Everybody complains,
but you'd be surprised how many re-enlist.'
– *James Garner*

Answers

1 *Flowers and Trees.* This Silly Symphonies production was the first colour cartoon film ever made

2 *Three Little Pigs*

3 Walter Elias Disney was born in Chicago on December 5 1901 and died in 1966

4 *Ice Age*

5 Jiminy Cricket

6 Huey, Dewey and Louis

7 *The Fox and the Hound*

8 *The Aristocats*

9 *Mickey's Christmas Carol*

10 *Bedknobs and Broomsticks*

11 Phil Harris, who also voiced many of Disney's cartoon characters including Baloo Bear in *The Jungle Book* (1967)

12 Orville, voiced by Jim Jordan

13 Alan Young (also the star of TV's *Mister Ed*)

14 Ed Wynn

15 *The Wise Little Hen* (1934)

'Art is for someone to figure out a hundred years from now.'
– *George Lucas*

IRISH CONNECTIONS & BEST OF BRITISH

Take 1

Irish Connection

1   John Ford directed Victor McLaglen in what 1935 movie about an IRA leader who, when betrayed by a local, wanted to emigrate?

2   It was a 1958 comedy about an Irish dustman starring John Gregson, Barry Fitzgerald and Noel Purcell. Can you name it?

3   Who played John Wayne's love interest in *The Quiet Man* (1952)?

4   James Cagney played a surgeon and a leader of the IRA in what 1959 movie, set in Dublin in 1921 ?

5   What movie, based on a novel by Michael Crichton, was filmed in Ireland in 1978 and starred Sean Connery, Donald Sutherland and Lesley Anne Down?

6   What Irish director made *The Company of Wolves* (1984)?

7   Martin Duffy made his debut film as writer/director in 1996. Can you name it?

8   Who played Stephen Dedalus in *A Portrait of the Artist as a Young Man* (1977), directed by Joseph Strick?

9   Who played Martin Cahill in *The General* (1998)?

10 Who played Michael Collins in the 1996 movie of the same title?

11 Name the 1997 crime-comedy set in Ireland, starring Brendan Gleeson as a hit man and Peter McDonald as his reluctant accomplice.

12 What 1998 road movie did Aisling Walsh direct, with Patricia Kerrigan and Anthony Connolly in the leads?

13 Eamon Morrissey and Stephen Brennan starred in what revved-up comedy drama from 1986 directed by Peter Ormrod?

14 Who directed the musical drama *The Commitments* (1991)?

15 *The Butcher Boy* (1997) was based on what Irish writer's novel?

Answers

1   *The Informer*

2   *Rooney*

3   Maureen O'Hara. The movie, directed by John Ford, also starred Barry Fitzgerald, Victor McLaglen and Ward Bond

4   *Shake Hands With the Devil*. The movie, directed by Michael Anderson, also starred Don Murray, Michael Redgrave and Cyril Cusack

5   *The First Great Train Robbery*

6   Neil Jordan

7   *The Boy From Mercury*. The movie starred James Hickey, Tom Courtenay and Rita Tushingham

8   Bosco Hogan

9   Brendan Gleeson

10 Liam Neeson. The movie also starred Julia Roberts, and was directed by Neil Jordan

11 *I Went Down*, directed by Paddy Breathnach

12 *Joyriders*

13 *Eat the Peach*

14 Alan Parker

15 Patrick McCabe

Ireland's first cinema opened in December 1909 in Mary Street, Dublin. The Volta, as it was called, was started by James Joyce after his sister Eva suggested that a cinema could make a lot of money.

Take 2

1   A moving tale chronicling the life of a Dublin artist and writer who was born with cerebral palsy. Can you name him and the movie from 1989?

2   Name the stars of *Nothing Personal* (1995), a movie about the Northern Ireland conflict?

3   It was a story about a mother whose son was in the IRA, and her fight for him when he was put into prison. Name this raw Northern Irish political drama from 1996.

4   In the 1967 film version of James Joyce's *Ulysses*, who played Leopold Bloom?

5   Who did the introductions to the three stories in *The Rising of the Moon* (1957)?

6   Actor Arthur Shields was the brother of which famous Irish actor?

7   Who played the two unlikely leads in *The Plough and the Stars* (1936), based on Sean O'Casey's classic play?

8   An action thriller set in Ireland in the 1980s starring Pierce Brosnan and Ray McNally, can you name this 1988 movie?

9   Robert Mitchum played a reluctant IRA recruit in what 1960 movie, set during World War II in Dublin?

10   Name the Laurence Olivier movie of 1962, shot mainly in Ireland, in which he played a teacher.

11   In what period romantic drama from 1992 did Tom Cruise play an Irishman?

12   Complete the title of David Lean's 1970 epic set in Ireland in 1916: *Ryan's _____*

13   Who was the male lead in *About Adam* (2000)?

14   In the movie *The Butcher Boy* (1998), who played the low-life drunk Jimmy the Skite?

15   Cillian Murphy and Colin Farrell starred in what Irish film from 2003?

Answers

1   The man was Christy Brown, played by Daniel Day Lewis, and the movie was *My Left Foot*. The movie also starred Ray McNally and Brenda Fricker

2   Ian Hart, John Lynch and Michael Gambon

3   *Some Mother's Son*, starring Helen Mirren

4   Milo O'Shea. Barbara Jefford played Molly Bloom

5   Tyrone Power. The movie was directed by John Ford

6   Barry Fitzgerald

7   Barbara Stanwyck and Preston Foster. The movie was directed by John Ford

8   *Taffin*, directed by Francis Megahy

9   *A Terrible Beauty*. The movie also starred Dan O'Herlihy, Richard Harris and Cyril Cusack

10   *Term of Trial*, directed by Peter Glenville and starring Simone Signoret, Terence Stamp and introducing Sarah Miles

11   *Far and Away*, directed by Ron Howard. Cruise's love interest was played by Nicole Kidman. The musical score was by Enya

12   *Ryan's Daughter*, starring Sarah Miles, Robert Mitchum, Trevor Howard, John Mills and Christopher Jones

13   Stuart Townsend. The movie also starred Kate Hudson

14   Patrick McCabe, the author of *The Butcher Boy*

15   *Intermission*

Production on Stanley Kubrick's movie *Barry Lyndon*, which started filming in 1973, had to be moved to England after Kubrick learned his name was on an IRA hit list for making a film showing English soldiers in Ireland.

Take 3

1. Who starred in *The Boxer* (1997)?

2. It was a political drama about the unlawful imprisonment of the Guildford Four. Can you name this 1993 movie?

3. What 1962 movie was based on a Brendan Behan play about a novice prison warden's moral dilemma about hanging, and starred Patrick McGoohan and Sylvia Syms?

4. What Irish actor played Renée Zellweger's father in *Cold Mountain* (2003)?

5. Who starred in *The Courier* (1988)?

6. Name the 1985 movie in which Liam Neeson played a Christian Brother who kidnapped a young boy to save him from a vindictive headmaster.

7. Name the 1982 film, directed by Neil Jordan, starring Stephen Rea, Alan Devlin and Veronica Quilligan.

8. Emily Watson and Robert Carlyle starred in what Alan Parker movie of 1999?

9. Name the director of *Intermission* (2003).

10. Who starred in *When Brendan Met Trudy* (2000)?

11. Name the second part of Roddy Doyle's trilogy brought to the screen. The first was *The Commitments* (1991) and the third was *The Van* (1996)?

12. Released in 1993, name the remake of a French film from 1962, based on a novel by Louis Pergaud, this time set in Ireland with screenplay by Colin Welland and produced by David Puttman, about warring village boys?

13. Which actor played the lead role in *King Arthur* (2004), filmed in Ireland?

14. What Irish actor played Lord Byron in *Gothic* (1986), directed by Ken Russell?

15. What was the name of the 1996 movie, penned by Wexford author and playwright Billy Roche, starring Richard Harris and Stephen Rea?

Answers

1   Daniel Day Lewis. The movie was directed by Jim Sheridan

2   *In the Name of the Father*. Gabriel Byrne was the executive producer

3   *The Quare Fellow*

4   Brendan Gleeson

5   Gabriel Byrne and Ian Bannen

6   *Lamb*. The movie also starred Ian Bannen

7   *Angel*

8   *Angela's Ashes*, based on Frank McCourt's bestselling book

9   John Crowley

10   Peter McDonald and Flora Montgomery

11   *The Snapper* (1993)

12   *The War of the Buttons*, directed by John Roberts

13   Clive Owen

14   Gabriel Byrne

15   *Trojan Eddie*

The first full-length Irish film with sound was *The Dawn* (1936), directed by Tom Cooper. The film focused on The War of Independence, and the actors consisted of actual veterans of the war.

Take 4

1   Which English actor played Paddy Doolan in *The Irishman* (1978)?

2   Which World War I movie of 1966 with spectacular aerial dog fights, filmed in Ireland, starred an American actor well known for his subsequent role as a cigar-chewing colonel in a popular TV series?

3   Which 1982 Oscar-winning epic movie starred Ben Kingsley and a youthful Daniel Day-Lewis ?

4   Who directed and scripted *The General* (1998)?

5   *Girl With Green Eyes* (1963), starring Peter Finch and Rita Tushingham, was filmed where in Ireland?

6   What profession did Patrick Bergin pursue before he became a movie star?

7   Where in Ireland was actor Kenneth Brannagh born?

8   Released in 1989, what was the movie debut of director Jim Sheridan?

9   Two of the performers picked up Oscars for *My Left Foot* (1989). Who were they?

10 What part of Dublin is director Neil Jordan from?

11 Where in Ireland did actor Stephen Rea grow up?

12 Who played the part of the Virgin Mary in the movie *King of Kings* (1961)?

13 How much did Pierce Brosnan earn for his role as James Bond 007 in *Die Another Day* (2003): $3.5 million, $9.5 million or $16.5 million?

14 Mia Farrow is the daughter of which famous Irish actress of the 1930s and 1940s?

15 What did the Irish Film Institute bestow on film and documentary maker Bob Quinn in 2001?

Answers

1   Michael Craig

2   *The Blue Max*, starring George Peppard

3   *Gandhi*, directed by Richard Attenborough

4   John Boorman

5   Dublin

6   He was a teacher

7   Belfast

8   *My Left Foot*

9   Brenda Fricker and Daniel Day-Lewis

10   Dalkey

11   Belfast

12   Siobhan McKenna

13    $16.5 million

14   Maureen O'Sullivan

15   A Lifetime Achievement Award

Only six weeks was spent on location in Ireland in 1952 filming *The Quiet Man*.
The scene that featured John Wayne kissing Maureen O'Hara for the first time
was a painful moment for the actress. As she moved to slap his face, the Duke
blocked the blow, breaking a bone in her hand.

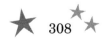

Take 5

British Connections

1. What was David Lean's job before he became a famous director?

2. Released in 1942, what was David Lean's directorial debut movie?

3. Who played Gustav Mahler in Ken Russell's *Mahler* (1974)?

4. Who played Colonel Brighton in *Lawrence of Arabia* (1962)?

5. Who directed *Bugsy Malone* (1976)?

6. Who produced such movies as *Midnight Express* (1978), *Chariots of Fire* (1981) and *The Killing Fields* (1984)?

7. Who played Laurence Olivier's daughter in *The Entertainer* (1960) and went on to marry him in real life?

8. Which versatile character actor from Scotland starred in such movies as *The Great Escape* (1963), *Mutiny on the Bounty* (1962), and *The Whistle Blower* (1987), and became a household name in the popular TV series *The Professionals*?

9. Who was the character actor from Scotland who appeared in such films as *Richard III* (1955), *Kidnapped* (1960), *The Reptile* (1966), and became very popular in the TV series *Dad's Army*?

10. Who played the bride in *The Bride of Frankenstein* (1935)?

11. Who were the famous brothers who had an important impact on British cinema with such movies as *The Private Life of Henry VIII* (1933), *The Private Life of Don Juan* (1934) and *Sanders of the River* (1935)?

12. Who was the eccentric character actress seen in *Blithe Spirit* (1945), and who portrayed Agatha Christie's Miss Marple in four movies. She also won an Oscar for *The V.I.Ps* (1963)?

13. Who directed *The Music Lovers* (1971)?

14. Who played Queen Elizabeth I in *Mary Queen of Scots* (1971)?

15. Where was Stan Laurel born?

Answers

1 He was a film editor and edited such films as *Pygmalion* (1938) and *49th Parallel* (1941)

2 *In Which We Serve*, co-directed by Noel Coward

3 Robert Powell

4 Anthony Quayle

5 Alan Parker

6 David Puttnam

7 Joan Plowright

8 Gordon Jackson

9 John Laurie

10 Elsa Lanchester

11 The Korda brothers – Alexander, Vincent and Zoltán

12 Margaret Rutherford

13 Ken Russell

14 Glenda Jackson

15 Ulverston, England on 16 June 1890

The British actor with the most screen credits to date is Christopher Lee.

Take 6

1   What well-known British rock star starred in *Ned Kelly* (1970)?

2   Name the 1971 British comedy in which Frankie Howerd played Lurcio and Michael Hordern played Ludicrus Sextus.

3   What was Sid James's first *Carry On* movie?

4   Who played the police officer in *Bunny Lake Is Missing* (1965)?

5   What 1960 movie was about ex-army officers recruited to rob a bank, and starred Jack Hawkins, Nigel Patrick and Richard Attenborough?

6   Name the romantic comic star of such movies as *I'm All Right Jack* (1959), *School for Scoundrels* (1960) and *Heavens Above* (1963)?

7   Michael Caine played a bespectacled intelligence man called Harry Palmer in three movies from 1965, 1966 and 1967. Can you name them?

8   What James Bond movie from 1964 had Honor Blackman as Pussy Galore?

9   Who wrestled naked with Oliver Reed in *Women in Love* (1969)?

10   Who played a young Mexican bandit in *The Singer Not The Song* (1960)?

11   Who played Titania in Peter Hall's *A Midsummer Night's Dream* (1968)?

12   Who played Indiana Jones's father in *Indiana Jones and The Last Crusade* (1989)?

13   In what 1962 movie did Julie Christie make her screen debut?

14   Can you name the highly successful director /producer team who happened to be brothers, whose films include *Carlton-Brown of the F.O.* (1959), *The Family Way* (1966), and *There's a Girl in my Soup* (1970)?

15   What movie from 1961, starring Dirk Bogarde, was one of the first successfully commercial movies to deal openly with homosexuality?

Answers

1   Mick Jagger

2   *Up Pompeii*

3   *Carry On Constable* (1960)

4   Laurence Olivier

5   *The League of Gentlemen*

6   Ian Carmichael

7   *The Ipcress File*, *Funeral in Berlin* and *Billion Dollar Brain*

8   *Goldfinger*

9   Alan Bates

10   Dirk Bogarde

11   Judi Dench

12   Sean Connery

13   *Crooks Anonymous*

14   Roy and John Boulting

15   *Victim*

The most versatile film maker yet has been Charlie Chaplin. In the movie *Limelight* (1952) he starred, directed, produced, edited, choreographed, composed, scripted and costume designed.

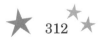

Take 7

1 Who directed *Chaplin* (1992)?

2 Who directed *This Sporting Life* (1963)?

3 Who was the male star of *The Thirty-Nine Steps* (1935)?

4 Complete the title of this Tom Courtenay movie from 1962: *The Loneliness of the* _____ _____ _____ .

5 Who played the bank manager in one of the most popular B-movies out of Britain, *Cash on Demand* (1963)?

6 Peter O'Toole played Henry II in two movies from 1964 and 1968, can you name them?

7 Who played D.H. Lawrence in *Priest of Love* (1981)?

8 Who played Renton in *Trainspotting* (1996)?

9 Anthony Hopkins played what famous writer in *Shadowlands* (1993)?

10 What English actor played opposite Gene Hackman in *Extreme Measures* (1997)?

11 Who played the photographer in *The Omen* (1976)?

12 How many parts did Alec Guinness play in the 1949 Ealing Comedy *Kind Hearts and Coronets*?

13 Who played Baron Munchausen in *The Adventures of Baron Munchausen* (1989)?

14 What was Pierce Brosnan's first Bond movie? In what year was it released?

15 Peter Jackson directed *Heavenly Creatures*. What English actress made her debut in this movie?

'I hated *Clueless* with a passion. I thought it would have been a really good film if someone had blown her head off at the end with a really huge gun. I mean, this rich bitch suddenly becomes charitable and then she's okay? And then there's the token black friend. It was so corrupt, so LA, I hated it.'
– *Ewan McGregor*

# Answers

1   Richard Attenborough

2   Lindsay Anderson

3   Robert Donat

4   *The Loneliness of the Long Distance Runner*

5   Peter Cushing

6   *Becket* and *The Lion in Winter*

7   Ian McKellen

8   Ewan McGregor

9   C.S. Lewis

10   Hugh Grant

11   David Warner

12   He played eight members of the D'Ascoyne clan

13   John Neville

14   *Goldeneye* (1995)

15   Kate Winslet

'I have a normal woman's body, I have a good pair of tits and a good arse.
If I didn't, I don't think I'd feel as attractive.'
– *Kate Winslet*

Take 8

1   Can you name the highly successful directors (and brothers) whose films include *Blade Runner* (1980), *The Hunger* (1983), *Thelma and Louise* (1991), *Enemy of the State* (1998) and *Gladiator* (2000)?

2   Alan Rickman and Juliet Stevenson starred in what 1990 movie, directed by Anthony Minghella?

3   Complete the title of this Kenneth Branagh movie from 1995: *In the Bleak _____*?

4   Released in 1957, what was the only non-Shakespearian movie that Laurence Olivier directed as well as acted in?

5   Can you name the Ken Russell movie from 1988 that was based on a Bram Stoker story?

6   A spy thriller by John Le Carré was turned into what 1969 movie, starring Christopher Jones, Ralph Richardson and Anthony Hopkins?

7   Who directed *The Third Man* (1949)?

8   Released in 1984, what was Ralph Richardson's final movie?

9   Who was the producer of the popular *Carry-On* movies?

10   Who played Scrooge in the 1951 movie of the same title?

11   Who played the female lead in George Bernard Shaw's *Androcles and the Lion* (1952)?

12   Who played Grace Kelly's husband in *Mogambo* (1953)?

13   In the movie *Never Let Go* (1960), who had his car stolen by Adam Faith for Peter Sellers?

14   In what 1959 movie did Hayley Mills make her debut?

15   Who starred as the gentle mild-mannered aristocrat in *The Shooting Party* (1984)?

The longest-running British movie series was the *Carry-On* series, which started in 1958. There were thirty in all, finishing in 1992. There has been talk of a new *Carry-On* film but it will entail a whole new cast.

# Answers

1   Tony and Ridley Scott

2   *Truly Madly Deeply*

3   *In the Bleak Midwinter*

4   *The Prince and the Showgirl*

5   *Lair of the White Worm*

6   *The Looking Glass War*

7   Carol Reed

8   *Greystoke, The Legend of Tarzan*

9   Peter Rogers

10 Alastair Sim

11 Jean Simmons

12 Donald Sinden

13 Richard Todd

14 *Tiger Bay*

15 James Mason

Most of the location for *Scott of the Antarctic* (1948) was in the Norwegian
town of Finse near the Arctic Circle.

Take 9

1   Who played Doctor Faustus in the 1967 movie of the same name, based on Christopher Marlow's play?

2   Where was Alfred Hitchcock born?

3   Who played Major Calloway in *The Third Man* (1949)?

4   Which English character actor played Baptista in Zeffirelli's *The Taming of the Shrew* (1966)?

5   Who played the aristocrat who is nannied by his butler in *The Remains of the Day* (1993)?

6   Who was the director of such movies as *Dr. Terror's House of Horrors* (1964), *Dracula Has Risen From the Grave* (1968), *The Ghoul* (1975), and was also the director of photography on films like *The Elephant Man* (1980) and *Cape Fear* (1991)?

7   Who directed *The Cook, The Thief, His Wife and Her Lover* (1989)?

8   Who played Jock Sinclair in *Tunes of Glory* (1960)?

9   Name the British actress who starred in such movies as *King Solomon's Mines* (1950), *From Here to Eternity* (1953) and *The King and I* (1956)?

10 Why is Daniel Radcliffe the most famous child actor ever?

11 Who played Nero in *Quo Vadis* (1951)?

12 Complete the title of David Lean's final movie: *A Passage ___ ___* (1984).

13 Who won an Oscar for her performance in the above movie?

14 Who played Lady Caroline Lamb in the 1972 movie of the same name?

15 Who played the photographer in *Blow-Up* (1967)?

'The reason an audience goes to see a film is often mysterious.'
– Neil Jordan

Answers

1. Richard Burton

2. London, England on 13 August 1899

3. Trevor Howard

4. Michael Hordern

5. James Fox

6. Freddie Francis

7. Peter Greenway

8. Alec Guinness

9. Deborah Kerr

10. He played Wizard Harry Potter in the *Harry Potter* movies

11. Peter Ustinov

12. *A Passage to India*

13. Peggy Ashcroft

14. Sarah Miles

15. David Hemmings

'I don't write anything I consider trashy. If anyone wants to have an opinion about it, that's absolutely fine with me.'
– *David Mamet*

Take 10

1   Who starred as the old woman in *The Whispers* (1966)?

2   Gary Oldman starred as what writer in *Prick Up Your Ears* (1987)?

3   Who played Isadora Duncan in the movie *Isadora* (1968)?

4   Who played Bill Sikes in *Oliver* (1968)?

5   Who was a success on Broadway in *The Killing of Sister George* and later repeated her role in the 1966 movie of the same name?

6   Who directed *Dirty Weekend* (1992)?

7   Who was the director of photography for *Lawrence of Arabia* (1962), *Doctor Zhivago* (1965), and *Battle of Britain* (1969)?

8   Who played Joy Adamson in *Born Free* (1965) and *The Lions Are Free* (1967)?

9   Ken Roach directed a movie about a young boy and his kestrel, can you name this movie from 1970?

10 Released in 1967, what was Vivien Leigh's last movie?

11 Name the actress who played Helen in *A Taste of Honey* (1961) and won a Bafta Award for her role?

12 Which popular comic actor in the 1950s and 1960s starred in such movies as *The Square Peg* (1958), *A Stitch in Time* (1963) and *The Early Bird* (1965)?

13 Who played Ophelia in Mel Gibson's *Hamlet* (1990)?

14 Who played Bob Hoskins' love interest in *The Long Good Friday* (1973)?

15 Name the 1964 war movie, set in Africa, about insurrection in a newly-formed state, and starring Richard Attenborough, Mia Farrow and Jack Hawkins.

'I'm typecast anyway – as me.'
– *Roger Moore*

Answers

1 Edith Evans

2 Joe Orton

3 Vanessa Redgrave

4 Oliver Reed

5 Beryl Reid

6 Michael Winner

7 Freddie Young

8 Virginia McKenna

9 *Kes*

10 *Ship of Fools*

11 Dora Bryan

12 Norman Wisdom

13 Helena Bonham-Carter

14 Helen Mirren

15 *Guns at Batasi*

'I've always wanted to be a spy, and frankly I'm a little surprised
that British Intelligence has never approached me.'
– *Elizabeth Hurley*

Take 11

1   Who played the explosives expert in *The Guns of Navarone* (1961)?

2   Who played 'Cutter' in *Gunga Din* (1939)?

3   Who directed *Lord of the Flies* (GB 1963)?

4   Can you name the black comedy from 1970, starring Richard Attenborough and Lee Remick, about stolen money that got buried in a coffin, based on Joe Orton's play?

5   Who was Jack Worthing in *The Importance of Being Earnest* (1952), based on Oscar Wilde's classic play?

6   *Brief Encounter* (1945) was based on a short play, *Still Life*. Who wrote the play?

7   Who played the teenage gangster 'Pinkie' in *Brighton Rock* (1947)?

8   Who played the dark stranger in *Brimstone and Treacle* (1982)?

9   *The Family Way* (1966) starred Hayley Mills and Hywel Bennett. Can you name the singer/songwriter with a string of hits, who wrote the score for this movie?

10 Who was the female star of *The Bitch* (1979), based on Jackie Collins' novel?

11 Which comic actor played Lord Wexmire in *Black Beauty* (1994)?

12 Who played Dustin Hoffman's wife in *Straw Dogs* (1971)?

13 In *Sense and Sensibility* (1995), who played Elinor Dashwood (and also wrote the screenplay based on the Jane Austin novel)?

14 Can you name the 1966 movie in which Joan Fontaine played a school mistress who discovered devil worshippers in rural England?

15 Name the 1959 movie about a small country that declared war on America in order to benefit from aid, starring Peter Sellers in three very different roles?

'What do you mean, heart attack?
You've got to have a heart before you can have an attack.'
– *Billy Wilder (on hearing that Peter Sellers had a heart attack)*

Answers

1   David Niven

2   Cary Grant

3   Peter Brook

4   *Loot*

5   Michael Redgrave

6   Noel Coward

7   Richard Attenborough

8   Sting

9   Paul McCartney

10 Joan Collins (Jackie's sister)

11 Peter Cook

12 Susan George

13 Emma Thompson

14 *The Witches*

15 *The Mouse That Roared*

'I'm looking for Commander James Bond, not an overgrown stunt man.'
– Ian Fleming (on Sean Connery)

Take 12

1   Who played Grand High Witch in *The Witches* (1989), based on the Roald Dahl classic children's book?

2   In what movie of 1982, does a black mamba slither up Oliver Reed's trouser leg?

3   A trilogy of stories about a car and its different owners starring Rex Harrison and Jeanne Moreau – can you name this 1964 movie?

4   In the 1971 movie version of *Under Milk Wood* by Dylan Thomas, who played Captain Cat?

5   Who directed and wrote *Local Hero* (1983)?

6   Who played the Indian doctor in *The Millionairess* (1961)?

7   Michael Crawford and Oliver Reed starred in what comedy thriller of 1967?

8   The film debut of director Stephen Frears starred Albert Finney as a bingo caller. Name this 1971 film set in lLiverpool.

9   Rik Mayall and Adrian Edmondson co-wrote and starred in this 1999 comedy. Can you name the film, which Edmondson also directed?

10 E.M. Forster's autobiographical novel was made into a movie about gay life in 1914 Cambridge starring James Wilby and Hugh Grant. Can you name the 1987 movie?

11 Name the black comedy from 1957, starring Peter Sellers, Terry Thomas, Peggy Mount and Dennis Price, about a TV host who's being blackmailed?

12 Julie Christie won an Oscar for what movie in 1965? (Dirk Bogarde and Laurence Harvey were her co-stars.)

13 Jeremy Irons played a politician who falls for his son's girlfriend (played by Juliette Binoche). Can you name this 1992 movie directed by Louis Malle?

14 Who played Jean Brodie in *The Prime of Miss Jean Brodie* (1969)?

15 Richard Burton played a vicious East End gangster in what crime drama of 1971?

Answers

1   Anjelica Huston

2   *Venom*

3   *The Yellow Rolls Royce*

4   Peter O'Toole

5   Bill Forsyth

6   Peter Sellers

7   *The Jokers*

8   *Gumshoe*

9   *Guest House Paradiso*

10   *Maurice*

11   *The Naked Truth*

12   *Darling*

13   *Damage*

14   Maggie Smith

15   *Villain*

'Acting is a kind of showing off and the best person to show off to is your wife.'
– Richard Burton

WHO SAID?

WHO SAID?

1 'I do nothing but work because I couldn't believe that an ugly schmuck like me could stay so lucky.'

2 'I am one of life's self-haters. I figure you've got to hate yourself if you've got any interest at all.'

3 'People don't credit me with much of a brain so why should I disillusion them?'

4 'I've always hated that James Bond. I'd like to kill him off.'

5 'I dress for women, I undress for men.'

6 'If you've got it, flaunt it.'

7 'I always made the same film, they just kept moving new leading ladies in front of me.'

8 'I hate acting, I'd rather direct.'

9 'I'm no actor – I just react to situations and what's said to me.'

10 'The length of a film should be directly related to endurance of the human bladder.'

11 'I don't want to be thought of as wholesome.'

12 'When choosing between two evils, I always like to try the one I've never tried before.'

13 'I wasn't fat, I was just Greek and Greeks are round, with big asses and big boobs.'

14 'Everyone seems to think I'm very ladylike, that I'm very cultured and intelligent. I drink a lot of Diet Coke and belch. I've been known to use the F-word. I've told a few dirty jokes. I arm-wrestle.'

15 'My mother always says, I'd rather see you naked than dead.'

1 Gene Hackman 2 Woody Allen 3 Sylvester Stallone 4 Sean Connery 5 Angie Dickenson 6 Mel Brooks 7 Robert Mitchum 8 Orson Welles 9 John Wayne 10 Alfred Hitchcock 11 Julie Andrews 12 Mae West 13 Jennifer Aniston 14 Helena Bonham Carter 15 Julianne Moore

WHO SAID?

1 'After doing *One Fine Day* (1996) and playing a pediatrician on *ER*, I'll never have kids. I'm going to have a vasectomy.'

2 'Actually, I really want to play Princess Leia. Stick some big pastries on my head. Now, that would be interesting.'

3 'I was in a restaurant the other night, and all the girls ignored me . . . it was so annoying.'

4 'When I look at a film of Kevin Costner's, I fall asleep out of boredom.'

5 'I love my name. I think it's great. I mean, Schwarzenegger – what's that?'

6 'My notion of a wife at 40 is that a man should be able to change her, like a bank note, for two 20s.'

7 'To succeed with the opposite sex, tell her you're impotent. She can't wait to disprove it.'

8 'In America, sex is an obsession; in other parts of the world it is a fact.'

9 'I never realised until lately that women were supposed to be the inferior sex.'

10 'The movie business divides women into ice queens and sluts, and there have been times I wanted to be a slut more than anything.'

11 'Women need a reason to have sex – men just need a place.'

12 'I believe that sex is one of the most beautiful, natural, wholesome things that money can buy.'

13 'Acting is a masochistic form of exhibitionism, not quite the occupation of an adult.'

14 'There is a certain combination of anarchy and discipline in the way I work.'

15 'There's only one way to have a happy marriage and as soon as I learn what it is I'll get married again.'

WHO SAID?

1   'If I wasn't an actor, I'd be a secret agent.'

2   'An actress can only play a woman. I'm an actor, I can play anything.'

3   'No one ever called me pretty when I was a little girl.'

4   'Failure is inevitable. Success is elusive.'

5   'Women should be obscene and not heard.'

6   'I love Mickey Mouse more than any woman I have ever known.'

7   'Everyone told me to pass on *Speed* because it was a "bus" movie.'

8   'Boredom is a great motivator.'

9   'Good judgement comes from experience. Sometimes, experience comes from bad judgement.'

10 'Being married means I can break wind and eat ice cream in bed.'

11 'Time you enjoy wasting, was not wasted.'

12 'Every man wishes to be wise, and they who cannot be wise are almost always cunning.'

13 'A lot of people are afraid to say what they want. That's why they don't get what they want.'

14 'I don't want people to know what I'm actually like. It's not good for an actor.'

15 'I want a man who's kind and understanding. Is that too much to ask of a millionaire?'

1 Elijah Wood 2 Whoopi Goldberg 3 Marilyn Monroe 4 Steven Spielberg 5 John Lennon 6 Walt Disney 7 Sandra Bullock 8 Uma Thurman 9 Christian Slater 10 Brad Pitt 11 John Lennon 12 Samuel L. Jackson 13 Madonna 14 Jack Nicholson 15 Zsa Zsa Gabor

WHO SAID?

1 'I've got rainbows up my ass, honey.'

2 'An epic is the easiest kind of movie to make badly.'

3 'I'm not an actress, I'm a phenomenon.'

4 'I shrivel up every time somebody mentions *Star Wars* to me.'

5 'I don't trust anybody who hasn't been self-destructive in some way.'

6 'Let's face it, the teeth are getting more English. Every day I look in the mirror and I see Austin Powers.'

7 'Beverly Hills has got a slum area, and it's called the rest of the world.'

8 'The first scary thing I learned to do as a child was to turn off the light.'

9 'Seeing Bambi's mom get killed is probably more frightening than anything in *Reservoir Dogs*.'

10 'I wanted to win an Oscar so I would get more scripts without other actors' coffee stains on them.'

11 'In most action movies, women are in the way.'

12 'Hollywood didn't kill Marilyn Monroe, it's the Marilyn Monroes who are killing Hollywood.'

13 'Everybody wants to be Cary Grant even I want to be Cary Grant.'

14 'Arnie's acted in plenty of movies but spoken less dialogue than any actor – except maybe Lassie.'

15 'Some of my best leading men have been horses and dogs.'

1 Judy Garland 2 Charlton Heston 3 Brigitte Bardot 4 Alec Guinness 5 Johnny Depp 6 Hugh Grant 7 Bob Hope 8 Steven Spielberg 9 Quentin Tarantino 10 Michael Caine 11 Arnold Schwarzenegger 12 Billy Wilder 13 Cary Grant 14 Robin Williams 15 Elizabeth Taylor

WHO SAID?

1 'For many years I could walk the streets unrecognised except by people who thought I was Dustin Hoffman.'

2 'You don't know a woman until you meet her in court.'

3 'When a man gives his opinion, he's a man. When a woman gives her opinion, she's a bitch.'

4 'Bad taste is simply saying the truth before it should be said.'

5 'The best films are best because of nobody but the director.'

6 'If I'm such a legend, why am I so lonely?'

7 'I did a picture in England once and it was so cold I almost got married.'

8 'I play John Wayne in every picture regardless of the character, and I've been doing all right, haven't I?'

9 'Sex is the biggest nothing of all time.'

10 'Being born with a beady-eyed sneer was the luckiest thing that ever happened to me.'

11 'I stopped believing in Santa Claus at an early age. Mother took me to see him in a department store, and he asked for my autograph.'

12 'I like the dead. They're so uncritical.'

13 'I started out as a lousy actress and have remained one.'

14 'Acting is an empty and useless profession.'

15 'Any prettier and it would have been called *Florence of Arabia*.'

1 Al Pacino 2 Woody Allen 3 Demi Moore 4 Mel Brooks 5 Roman Polanski 6 Judy Garland 7 Shelley Winters 8 John Wayne 9 Andy Warhol 10 Lee Van Cleef 11 Shirley Temple 12 Tom Baker 13 Brigitte Bardot 14 Marlon Brando 15 Noel Coward

WHO SAID?

Lord of the Rings Trilogy

1   'We work so well with Pete because he understands Hobbits, because he is a Hobbit. He has so many Hobbit qualities to him.'

2   'It's that unconditional love (of Sam's) that says whatever you do or wherever you go I'm there for you.'

3   'Peter Jackson is a fantastic guy! He's cool like an Elf, has the heart of a Hobbit and is crazy as a Wizard.'

4   'I thought: I can go to New Zealand for a few weeks, be in one or a few amazing scenes and then go home and know that I've been in one of the greatest movies of all time.'

5   'To play one of the main characters in it, it's not the kind of thing you don't do. I can't actually think of another job that I'd rather do.'

6   'Orlando Bloom is a terrific actor. He comes to me a lot for advice on how to do different scenes. And he laughs at all of my jokes.'

7   'Frodo has just got a spirit, you know? That's what I love about him. He's very alive and very lively. His spirit, the light that's in him, is what holds him together.'

8   'It is in Bree that the Hobbits really get the feeling that they've left their secure home and gone on a dangerous adventure. It's truly a moment of "We're not in Kansas anymore, Toto."'

9   'I won't miss having to stand for two hours at 4.30 a.m. and have freezing cold glue applied to my feet. I won't miss two-hour drives to work or long, long, long days sitting in my trailer waiting . . . waiting . . . waiting. But I would do it all again tomorrow.'

10   'It's not us who are short, it's all the other guys who are tall!'

1 Dominic Monaghan (Merry)   2 Elijah Wood (Frodo)   3 Orlando Bloom (Legolas) 4 John Rhys-Davies (Gimli)   5 Billy Boyd (Pippin)   6 Sir Ian McKellen (Gandalf) 7 Elijah Wood   8 Sean Astin (Sam)   9 Dominic Monaghan   10 Billy Boyd

★ 332 ★★

Appendices

Academy Awards for Best Picture

2004	The Lord of the Rings: The Return of the King
2003	Chicago
2002	A Beautiful Mind
2001	Gladiator
2000	American Beauty
1999	Shakespeare in Love
1998	Titanic
1999	The English Patient
1996	Braveheart
1995	Forrest Gump
1994	Schindler's List
1993	Unforgiven
1992	The Silence of the Lambs
1991	Dances with Wolves
1990	Driving Miss Daisy
1989	Rain Man
1988	The Last Emperor
1987	Platoon
1986	Out of Africa
1985	Amadeus
1984	Terms of Endearment
1983	Gandhi
1982	Chariots of Fire
1981	Ordinary People
1980	Kramer Vs Kramer
1979	The Deer Hunter
1978	Annie Hall
1977	Rocky
1976	One Flew Over the Cuckoo's Nest
1975	The Godfather Part II
1974	The Sting
1973	The Godfather
1972	The French Connection
1971	Patton
1970	Midnight Cowboy
1969	Oliver!
1968	In the Heat of the Night
1967	A Man for All Seasons
1966	The Sound of Music

Appendices

Academy Awards for Best Picture

1965	My Fair Lady
1964	Tom Jones
1963	Lawrence of Arabia
1962	West Side Story
1961	The Apartment
1960	Ben-Hur
1959	Gigi
1958	The Bridge on the River Kwai
1957	Around the World in 80 Days
1956	Marty
1955	On the Waterfront
1954	From Here to Eternity
1953	The Greatest Show on Earth
1952	An American in Paris
1951	All About Eve
1950	All the King's Men
1949	Hamlet
1948	Gentleman's Agreement
1947	The Best Years of Our Lives
1946	The Lost Weekend
1945	Going My Way
1944	Casablanca
1943	Mrs. Miniver
1942	How Green Was My Valley
1941	Rebecca
1940	Gone with the Wind
1939	You Can't Take It With You
1938	The Life of Emile Zola
1937	The Great Ziegfeld
1936	Mutiny on the Bounty
1935	It Happened One Night
1934	**There was no Oscar ceremony that year**
1933	Cavalcade
1932	Grand Hotel
1931	Cimarron
1930	All Quiet on the Western Front
1929	Broadway Melody
1928	Wings

Appendices

Bafta Awards for Best Film

2004	Lord of the Rings: The Return of the King
2003	The Pianist
2002	Lord of the Rings: The Fellowship of the Ring
2001	Gladiator
2000	American Beauty
1999	Shakespeare in Love
1998	The Full Monty
1997	The English Patient
1996	Sense and Sensibility
1995	The Usual Suspects
1994	Four Weddings and a Funeral
1993	Schindler's List
1992	Howard's End
1991	The Commitments
1990	Goodfellas
1989	Dead Poets Society
1988	The Last Emperor
1987	Jean de Florette
1986	A Room with a View
1985	The Purple Rose of Cairo
1984	The Killing Fields
1983	Educating Rita
1982	Gandhi
1981	Chariots of Fire
1980	The Elephant Man
1979	Manhattan
1978	Julia
1977	Annie Hall
1976	One Flew Over the Cuckoo's Nest
1975	Alice Doesn't Live Here Anymore
1974	Lacombe Lucien
1973	La Nuit Américaine
1972	Cabaret
1971	Sunday Bloody Sunday
1970	Butch Cassidy and the Sundance Kid
1969	Midnight Cowboy
1968	The Graduate
1967	A Man for All Seasons Best British Film: A Man for All Seasons

Appendices

Bafta Awards for Best Film

1966   Who's Afraid of Virginia Woolf?
Best British Film: The Spy that came in from the Cold

1965   My Fair Lady
Best British Film: The Ipcress File

1964   Dr. Strangelove or How I Learned to Stop Worrying and Love the Bomb

Best British Film:
Dr. Strangelove or How I Learned to Stop Worrying and Love the Bomb

1963   Tom Jones
Best British Film: The Servant

1962   Laurence of Arabia
Best British Film: Lawrence of Arabia

1961   Ballad of a Soldier / The Hustler
Best British Film: A Taste of Honey

1960   The Apartment
Best British Film: Saturday Night and Sunday Morning

1959   Ben-Hur
Best British Film: Sapphire

1958   Room at the Top
Best British Film: Room at the Top

1957   The Bridge on the River Kwai
Best British Film:
The Bridge on the River Kwai

1956   Gervaise
Best British Film: Reach for the Sky

1955   Richard III
Best British Film: Richard III

1954   The Wages of Fear
Best British Film: Hobson's Choice

1953   Jeux Interdits
Best British Film: Geneviève

1952   The Sound Barrier
Best British Film: The Sound Barrier

1951   Là Ronde
Best British Film: Lavender Hill Mob

1950   All About Eve
Best British Film: The Blue Lamp

1949   The Bicycle Thief
Best British Film: The Third Man

1948   Hamlet
Best British Film: The Fallen Idol

1947   The Best Years of Our Lives
Best British Film: Odd Man Out